To Gaspar Gatlos Gibbs

Sam Noto,
A Life In Jazz

I hope you enjoy this as much as I did in writing it!

Joey Giambra

Joey Giambra

DEDICATION

Dedicated to the memory of Nick Menza (July 23, 1964 – May 21, 2016), the great American drummer born in Munich, West Germany, to Rose Yarusso and iconic tenor saxophonist Don (Red) Menza, then a member of the renowned German orchestra of Max Greger.

Munich is not Efner Street nor is it Busti Avenue on Buffalo's lower West Side where Don Menza and Sam Noto grew up amid a dormant canal, basso profondo tugs, and the lonesome atonality of trains.

Ultimately, that atonality would accompany them and countless of their neighborhood musicians on their way to international fame.

CONTENTS

ACKNOWLEDGMENTS

A special thanks to the Sportsmen's Americana Music Foundation in Buffalo, New York, for their generous support of this project.

SAM NOTO, A JAZZ LIFE

Many who will read these pages and see the word "sideman" will know its meaning, and many will not. In the 1930s, 40s, and 50s "sidemen" were musicians: drums, piano, bass, guitar, reed, or brass players in jazz bands or jazz orchestras of the day. Each was chosen to garner a universal blend. Some became soloists in those musical aggregations, as did Sam Noto, a one-time sideman and jazz trumpeter born in Buffalo, New York, on April 17, 1930, who became an international trumpet star.

After earning accolades as a player in Buffalo in the late 40s and early 50s, Sam Noto was called to substitute in the Stan Kenton Orchestra, who were appearing in a downtown Buffalo theatre. Sam played the gig and was hired as a sideman. He evolved to soloist and Kenton's lead trumpeter. That spawned a career spanning seven decades and included tenures with Count Basie, Louie Bellson, and Woody Herman. In small groups he excelled with tenor men Dexter Gordon, Al Cohn, and Joe Romanello; with Buffalo expatriates Don Menza, Larry Covelli, and alto man Joe (Mouse) Bonati. Noto and Bonati played in Las Vegas Casino show bands and also recorded. In Vegas Sam and the jazz trumpeter Red Rodney, depicted in Clint Eastwood's movie Bird, co-led and recorded "Super Bop" with their sensational group. In later years Sam left for Canada to join valve trombonist's Rob McConnell's iconic Boss Brass with whom he also recorded.

Sam's Early Life

Early in the 1920s, Louis Noto and Santina Territo lived in the province of Caltanisetta, Sicily, in the village of Sutera, unknown to each other. Soon, like many seeking a better life in the New World they immigrated—separately and at different times—to Birmingham, Alabama where they subsequently met. Louis worked on a plantation, where life was a vicious cycle of turbulence, desolation, and grief in a dreadful setting. He and a brother who had immigrated to Birmingham earlier mined coal and stoked furnaces in a steel plant. For Santina, Louis, and his brother, white privilege was not in their sphere, nor was the American Dream. They and the rest of the Sicilian community were socially classified as black, or people of color. Like Birmingham's blacks, they knew their communities would remain the perpetual underclass, isolated from Southern white America. Little did Louis and Santina know that in two decades their exceptional third child, Sam, would have such an impact on America's jazz scene.

The Notos, with their children Gabriele (Bill) and Joseph, left Alabama for Buffalo, New York, to live at 69 Busti Avenue on that city's lower West Side. Sam was born there in 1930, followed by siblings Rose Ann and Charles. Also born around that time were Sam Scamacca, Angelo (Billy) Licata, and Anthony Sorrento—future gifted clarinetists. Sam, now an octogenarian, lives with his family in Fort Erie, Canada, a stone's throw from the streets of Buffalo where he acquired his formative musicianship.

Today, in a world of electronic annoyances, many think a bugler on a horse is playing a trumpet. No. That is a physical impossibility. A trumpet has three valves, and to play it two hands are needed. Like the bugle, it has a mouthpiece, but it also has various metal tubing, and unlike the bugle it has a centuries-long history. To play a trumpet, the air that produces the notes and sounds must be blown through almost closed lips. One needs a proper embouchure that creates a buzz, a vibration in the air column. Sam Noto has noted that trumpet players deal with mouthpiece problems, diet, and stamina. After shedding that light, let's explore some of Sam's famous contemporaries.

Sam's Contemporaries

Louis Armstrong brought the trumpet to global prominence during the Roaring Twenties. Bunny Berigan and Louis Prima reigned in the 30s, followed by Harry James, Dizzy Gillespie, 'Fats' Navarro, Miles Davis, Clifford Brown, Chet Baker, Clark Terry, and Maynard Ferguson. From the 30s to the 60s, scores of Italian American musicians lived not far from Sam's birthplace, including John Sedola, Hank D'Amico, Sam Mineo, Angelo Lorenzo, Don Menza, Don Paladino, Tom Ingrassia, Joe Gustaferro, Joe Bonati, Tony Ragusa, and Angelo Callea. Many would become sidemen, and some would become jazz artists in America's big-name bands. Among them lived classical piano genius, Leonard Pennario, with whom violin virtuoso Jascha Heifitz chose many times to perform. From Trenton Avenue came Dan Trimboli, a brilliant clarinetist, who in the late 40s taught music at Hutchinson Central High School before moving to Manhattan. There, Leonard Bernstein and the New York Philharmonic selected him to perform a symphonic piece for alto saxophone written by French composer Darius Milhaud.

By the late 30s, early 40s, the Notos lived at 179 Busti Avenue before moving to 156 West Avenue. By age 13 Sam was performing menial tasks on Virginia Street at The Marlowe, aka The Bug House, a movie theater rife with double features, westerns, cartoons, newsreels, coming attractions, and predictable serials. There, for twelve cents in the darkness of a Saturday afternoon, Sam and others (including me) took refuge on horses and lived vicariously as cowboys and fantasized that we fought outlaws with John Wayne or persevered in a watery submarine with Cary Grant and John Garfield. Often, we were imaginary guests in the never-before seen homes of Henry Aldrich or Andy Hardy. In the light of day we were never anywhere but in the sluggish marrow of our young minds, and in the climate of the time.

In 1943 my family was living at 73 Efner Street, a narrow red cobblestone path in the shadow of City Hall. At 55 Efner were the Calabreses; a family with many boys. The second youngest of these was Vincent, nicknamed Jabber, who, though he was older, befriended me. He was a trumpet player with a fat, distinctive

3

sound. I recall him playing "I'll Be Seeing You," a timeless song from 1938 that ultimately became a national psalm for America's armed forces during World War II. Written by Irving Kahal and Sammy Fain, that haunting melody personified sad and voluminous lost connections to loved ones. Hearing its poignant, indelible lyric filled my young heart. Jabber's playing made me aspire to learn the trumpet, though I knew it was economically impossible.

In 1943 as a ten-year-old first-generation American entrepreneur, I shined shoes on the feet of US servicemen and embraced the world of commerce in Spike Sullivan's, an old Georgia Street saloon. It was the last bastion of alcohol in a once-thriving Gaelic zone near the former Erie Barge Canal and a rusted bridge to Lake Erie. Due to Spike's compassion, we earned coins and nicknames. Carlo, Vinnie, and Tony became Coogan, Murphy, and Smitty. Me? I was Joey, and that I would remain. With two dollars in assorted coins I rented a trumpet from Miss Rodenhoffer, our affable music teacher at P.S. #2 on the Lower Terrace. It was mine for 52 weeks, and she was my friend for life. I shall never forget her.

Later, my family moved to 203 Busti Avenue. It was one hundred and thirty-four digits from 69—Sam Noto's birthplace—and twenty-eight digits from his later flat at 175. Busti was a large asphalt-paved thoroughfare lined with massive trees under which one could live. Unlike Efner's sparse, plain wooden light standards, Busti's were numerous, metallic, and shaded green. Multi-colored autos never before seen by me produced different sounds and at least one seminal sight: women drivers smoking cigarettes. Here, where once boiled cabbage ruled, the aroma of meatballs, sausage, and spare ribs in sauce filled the air.

But it was not until 1949 that I first heard Sam Noto at the West Mohawk Street YWCA. I was sixteen and still hadn't met him, but he was preceded by his reputation. He and gifted tenor man Joe Campagna were wailing on "Cherokee." Noto's sound was full, fleet, creative, and luminous. On the ballad "I Can Dream, Can't I?" (also by Kahal and Fain) his heartfelt playing, his stance, a cigarette dangling as he caressed his treasured three-valves, struck this fledgling. That sensitive moment allowed me to absorb a jazz aura; a night that embodied the memorable enormity of a young musician, one destined for fame.

The following year Sam Noto and I became friends. Soon afterwards, through a quirk of fate, Noto replaced trumpeter extraordinaire Conte Candoli in Stan Kenton's Orchestra. Though Dizzy Gillespie influenced Noto's early playing, Candoli was also one of Sam's favorites.

ORIGINS

Sam Noto tells me it all began in 1932 on Busti Avenue, when he, a gregarious and precocious two-year-old was in his high chair. He was restless, and from that lofty perch next to the family's wind-up Victrola he made much noise. In later years his mother often reminded him that as a child he had done that repeatedly, and the only thing that would make him stop was music in the form of a 78 rpm record that Mrs. Noto placed on the Victrola. Sam says, "I was in my glory listening in earnest to Jack Payne and his BBC English dance band playing 'Now's the Time to Fall in Love.' "

At this point in an early interview for this book, Sam sang the opening lyrics: "Tomatoes are cheaper, / potatoes are cheaper, / now's the time to fall in love." But when the record wore down and the band wobbled, and the vocalist quivered, diminished to a non-recognizable dynamic, Sam's restlessness surfaced. Sam said, "The machine needed further winding. I decided I didn't like it sounding like that, so I started crying again."

When that happened, one of his three siblings was quickly summoned to what immigrant families called "the talking machine." When the machine was rewound it regained its stamina and was brought back to life. A new existence was given the British vocalist and the band. They were alive, and were heard loud, clear, and at the proper pitch. "Now's the Time to Fall in Love" became Sam's favorite. This drama occurred daily. Sam doesn't know how that recording made its way into the Noto household, but it certainly made the future musician happy. Sam says, "There was a 'wah-wah' kind of trumpet solo, something like that; that kind of thing on the record. I was really intrigued by it. I loved that tune and the trumpet solo, so I'd listen, and I'd be cool."

Potatoes are cheaper,
Tomatoes are cheaper,
Now's the time to fall in love,
Why the butcher, the baker,
The old candlestick maker
Gave their prices a downward shove,
Grab yourself someone to fry your eggs and bacon, she
Can live just like a queen
On what you're makin',
You'll find in some kind o' trouble
You're better off double,
Now's the time to fall in love
Sweets are much cheaper
Movie seats are much cheaper
Now's the time to fall in love
The talkies seem tender to make her surrender
You should take advantage
Of when the picture's over
Take her where it's quiet
Just remember what the hero did and try it
You're not a Coleman or Gable
But do what you're able
Now's the time to fall in love.

Al Sherman and *Al Lewis*

Later, Eddie Cantor's recording of this song became young Sam's favorite. It was a huge hit, but Bing Crosby's 1932 recording, "Brother Can You Spare a Dime" most epitomizes the way it was for the Notos and others of that era.

And so it went. After many playings of Jack Payne's recording the family, tired of winding, allowed two-year-old Sam to wind the Victrola himself. He would wind it so tight that it broke, and after his father repaired it Sam would repeat the process. At the time they lived on Busti Avenue near Georgia Street, next to

Tagliarino's Dairy. Sam says, "I remember we never left the house through the front door, always the side door. There was a big driveway that led to the back of a barn next to the home of the Tagliarinos who owned the dairy. There was hay in the barn, lots of hay and horses that Mr. Matthew Tagliarino attached to a wagon to deliver his milk. As a toddler I remember that distinctly. I'd come out through that side door and in the driveway there was a Tagliarino boy whose name was Joe. I was about his age, maybe two, two and a half, and we went into his father's barn to play and jump around in the hay. My two older brothers, Bill and Joe, would come in as well, and be in on the shenanigans."

But in that time, while two-year-old Joe Tagliarino and the young Noto brothers romped in the hay, the Great Depression, now in its zenith, was delivering disturbance nationally. Lives were turned upside down. Unemployment was at an all-time high and the wealth, opulence, joy, and forced gayety of the 1920s had all but disappeared. People marveled as Amelia Earhart flew solo across the Atlantic Ocean and mourned when the kidnapped 20-month-old son of Charles and Anne Lindbergh was found dead. Jack Sharkey beat Max Schmeling for the world heavyweight championship. Radio City Music Hall opened, and Franklin Delano Roosevelt was elected President.

Sam says, "You must remember what comes to mind from that period, now that I think back on it, my father had a brand-new car. It was a Ford. He was working in construction and he must have paid about three hundred, maybe two hundred and seventy-five dollars; no, I remember he paid three hundred and twenty-five dollars for that car. He was so proud of it. He parked it on our side of the driveway across from the dairy. I would jump in there and play. A lot of kids did. I'd grab the steering wheel and make believe I was driving and stuff like that. Then, the Great Depression was in full bloom. My father lost his construction job, and unable to find another, he couldn't make the car payments and it was repossessed; they came and took it away. That was a sad thing for my father, and for us kids too, because now we couldn't play in the car anymore. My father was unhappy, as were millions of others who couldn't find work. Lacking income, we went on welfare. We couldn't pay the rent, we didn't have food, the whole thing. I'm sure many families went through that. I know lots of people, lots of families from the West Side went through that."

As Sam was getting older the family moved from Busti Avenue to Seventh Street, or, as Sam says, "Maybe it was Trenton Avenue. I know we lived there once, and once on Efner Street. The only reason I know the names of those streets is because my mother told me about all the times we had to move and how she and my father, bugged about not working, tried to remain as stable as possible."

Life during the Depression was hard on everyone. The Notos took a wagon to the welfare building downtown to get food; chunks of cheese, flour, butter, and all those necessities came from the welfare authorities. Sam says, "We'd put everything in the wagon, wheel it to where we lived at the time, and brought it in the house, the whole thing. I think there was some help in paying the rent and utilities."

Sam further says, "Keep in mind, those early welfare years of my life on the lower West Side were rough ones. That's all we knew. We were kids who played in the street and had a good time, but our parents were hurting because they couldn't do right by us. My father was always bugged; angry because of the work situation. We lived at 69 Seventh Street across from P.S. #73. Life was different, momentous, and vibrant."

Though many neighboring denizens were poor, Sam's days were filled with great camaraderie. There was comic relief from many characters. Sam relishes stories about the Catalanos, Arthur (Arturo) and Joe, who lived vicariously as Perry Como and Frank Sinatra, and whom Sam befriended. Sam says, "They inverted English and spoke differently. Nickel became nyookul, dime was dyoom or dimmerschnap, etc., etc. A few doors from the school there was Rossitto's Grocery Store, owned by my friend Carmen Rossitto's father." The Notos, when able, bought varied inexpensive goods there.

Sam told me, "Carmen and I hung out. One day we were on the corner where Seventh Street turns to become Court Street not far from the firehouse. There was a big building there, like a trucking company, some kind of business, and it had a big sturdy metal garage door. Carmen and I played handball against that door. So, one day, it was cold, we're playing, and Carmen hits something called a 'black bottom.' I went for the ball. As I did, I fell on my face and broke a tooth. I must have looked hilarious because Carmen was laughing his head off. When I fell I started crying because the cold air hit the tooth and it was painful. Carmen helped me look for the tooth and we found it! Crying, I brought it home and told my mother. Of course, there was no money for a dentist to fix the problem. So, I went through all of my years with a broken tooth. I was twelve years old when I started playing trumpet, and until recently I still had the broken tooth.

"Along the way I remember professionals with whom I played all saying the same thing: the reason I could play all these high notes and have great strength and chops was because of the broken tooth. I met my good friend Guido Basso, the great, legendary Canadian jazz trumpet player years ago when we were in Louie Bellson's big band. Much later, we were in Toronto with Rob McConnell's Boss Brass. One night, Guido is next to me on the bandstand. I turn around and I see him hitting his mouth with his mouthpiece. I said, 'What are you doing, man?' He said, 'I want to break my tooth so I could play strong like you.' He is a funny cat. I always laugh when I think of that."

SEVENTH STREET, THE LOWER WEST SIDE

Sam relates, "During those early years a bunch of us guys, we had like a gang so to speak in an alley behind Seventh Street. I think it was Utely Alley. We'd run and jump on rooftops and see who could jump the highest. We'd raid neighborhood fruit trees, and people with shovels would chase us. Then, if the people whose fruit we stole saw us on the street and recognized us, they told our parents. So when you got home, your father would give you a whipping for stealing. But we, me included, we'd never learn. We'd go back and do it again. We lacked material things—bikes, nothing with which to play."

As mentioned earlier, to amuse themselves Sam and his friends played street games: Buck Buck, How Many is Up, Kick the Can, You're It, and Hopscotch. Sam says, "When the delivery guy brought doughnuts to a store one of us would keep an eye on him, while outside others would raid the truck. Later, we'd eat doughnuts till we were sick to our stomachs."

When the Notos moved to West Avenue Sam attended P.S. #76 on Elmwood Avenue. He says, "My first year there someone asked if anyone wanted to play a musical instrument. I said that I liked the trumpet and wanted to play one. I was told that for two dollars I could rent one for a year. I went home and told my mother, 'Ma, the school wants to rent me a trumpet. Can you get two dollars? I need it. I want to get the trumpet.' She said they couldn't afford to give me two dollars. But a friend of the family,

Mike Polito, said, 'I've got a trumpet in my closet. I'll let you use it.' "

Mike Polito brought Sam the trumpet and Sam started playing it at home. Then he brought it to school and began taking lessons from Mr. Bish, the music teacher. He was learning scales, and all the rudiments attached to early study. Sam says, "When I'm home, instead of doing homework I'd practice my trumpet. When I got my report card my grades were down. Ironically, Mike Polito, who would later sponsor me at St. Anthony's Church where I was confirmed, said 'that's it!' and he retrieved the trumpet. Oh man, that was so very, very hurtful because I was really starting to dig that horn, and I started crying.

"The Great Depression had ended by then, and when my father came home from his construction job my mother told him the whole story. She said, 'His grades are bad, so Mike took back the trumpet.' My father looked down at me and said, 'C'mon.' "

Sam and his father walked towards downtown to Court and Pearl streets where stood Denton, Cottier, and Daniels, a grand, classic music store. In its display window were many beautiful, brand-new musical instruments: clarinets, bright shiny gold-plated saxophones, trombones, and trumpets. A price tag on a trumpet indicated its cost: eighty-nine dollars. Sam's father stared sadly at the numbers. "I can't do it, Sam. We don't have that much money."

Ultimately, Sam's parents scraped up the two dollars, and Sam rented the school trumpet for the year. Later, one of his father's coworkers, privy to the Denton, Cottier and Daniels episode, said that he had a trumpet in his closet that wasn't doing anything. "He gave it to my father who brought it home, and all of a sudden I really owned a trumpet. It was one of those long, skinny ones, and it was made in France. I don't remember how it played, but I loved it. It was my trumpet. I took some lessons from Pat Vastola, who was known as Patty Van, and who at one time led the band at Chez Ami on Delaware Avenue. During a lesson he told me a joke. He said, 'Answer this riddle: if two trumpet players were on the street and had an argument, a fight, where would they hit each other?' I said, 'in the mouth.' He said, 'No, they'd pat each other on the ass; it's a lot more fun.' "

Soon, Sam was able to play Stardust, and did so at a wedding at the Virginia Hall near the Marlowe movie theater. He received fifty cents and all the peanuts and cookies he could eat. Sam says, "You might say it was my first trumpet gig."

After graduating from grammar school, to appease his older brother, Bill, and his parents who didn't want him to pursue his music, he studied printing at Burgard High School, but he still played the trumpet. Soon, Sam thought he knew how to play "Pennies from Heaven," a pretty song from a 1936 Bing Crosby movie of the same name. Emboldened, Sam went to the Orchid Lounge, a Black Rock saloon where Joe Guercio, a piano player a bit older than he had a band. Sam says, "He let me play 'Pennies' and I messed it up. Joe stopped the band and told me to go home and practice. I was so embarrassed; I left and vowed to learn that tune. I went to the Grosvenor Library with music paper to copy all of 'Pennies' notes. I did and played that tune constantly for an entire week until I had it down. I said, 'Hey, this is all right.' I returned to the Orchid Lounge. Joe Guercio saw me. The expression on his face was, 'Oh no, he's here again.' I asked him if I could play 'Pennies from Heaven.' Guercio said, 'No, we're playing 'That Old Black Magic'.' I was screwed again! Amazing.

"Many years later, that same Joe Guercio was the musical director at the Las Vegas Hilton and subsequently Elvis Presley's conductor. He went from playing an out of tune upright piano in a Black Rock saloon to becoming Elvis Presley's long-time musical conductor. When I worked for him in Vegas I mentioned what went down at the Orchid Lounge years ago, but he didn't remember."

Sam Noto says, "That whole trumpet thing had to start when I entered P.S. #76. I was about twelve years old, my first year in the band with Mr. Bish. I did that and practiced and practiced until graduating in 1944. At the time I fell in love with Barbara Fabian, a beautiful girl who played alto saxophone in the band. I didn't know how to approach her. I was too bashful to talk to her, but I had this big crush on her. There were a few other band guys with crushes on her. We were kids, 12 – 13, and we'd walk her home every day wondering which one of us she liked, and which one of us would end up with her."

Fourteen-year-old Sam Noto never saw the love of his young life again. He wanted to go to Grover Cleveland High School or to Hutchinson Central to take advantage of Hutch's music course. His brother, Bill, decided he should go to a vocational school so he would have something to fall back on. Sam told them, "I want to be a musician, a trumpet player." His father agreed with Bill.

Bill said, "What if you break your tooth again and can't play anymore, then what?"

So, Sam went to Burgard Vocational on Kensington Avenue to take up printing, but he still played his trumpet.

MR. WEIS AND THE ONE O' CLOCK JUMP

Sam says, "Early on at Burgard I had a few years of experience on the trumpet. I was in the band, and in a trumpet trio with Chuck Rizzone and Joe Hunold. We performed in the morning assembly. I was getting a reputation as a player from those who liked that stuff. Chuck and I took the same Broadway bus every day to get to the school annex; I think that's where we went for a year or two. I'd play my trumpet on the bus, but he wouldn't. To the macho guys, the sports guys at school, I was a nerd. All I did was play trumpet; no sports. But in grammar school, while in the band, I did play basketball. Once, at halftime, I left the locker room in my basketball uniform to play my trumpet in the band. We won the championship that year. I was on the C team, the shortest of the A, B, and C teams.

"While I was at Burgard, my brother, Bill, who, by this time was a musician playing drums, said, "I met this guy, Andy James from South Buffalo somewhere who is forming a band and I'm in it. I asked him if you could be in the trumpet section and he said yes.""

I said, "Oh yeah! Oh, yeah!"

Sam went on, "I went to a rehearsal. Mike Scime played first trumpet. Charlie Vastola played second, and I played third. It was a lot of fun, me in Andy James orchestra. That meant I was in my first dance band! We had a gig coming up on New Year's Eve, and I had a solo to play an arrangement on 'One O' Clock Jump,' a blues in B flat. It only had chord symbols, no melody notes. I took it to Mr. Weis, my high school music teacher who wrote out a jazz solo for me. I practiced, practiced, and practiced, and when I played it at rehearsal I knocked everybody out. Oh, boy, after that I said, 'These Andy James guys are jazz players,' and I started digging that. Then I began changing the solo, a little here, a little there, putting different notes; creating my own melody, and that's when I began learning about chords, chord symbols, and different scales."

Mr. Weis, who was a trumpet player and a noted pianist, took an interest in Sam because he saw a youngster totally interested in music and desirous of becoming a serious trumpet player. Along with the regular school band practice Sam had big band practice. Kenny Greene was the drummer. His brother, Jimmy Greene, led the Sunday afternoon jam sessions at the Colored Local, or Colored Musicians Club as it's now called. Sam remembers Kenny as being, "A good guy. We were tight. We had a great time and always got along. Mr. Weis would keep me after school and give me what you might call free lessons: diaphragm breathing, that kind of thing, and his music theory, and extensive knowledge. Then, suddenly I wanted to quit school, and that meant quitting the band. But before I did, my brother Bill got me on Andy James's band.

"Andy James was an alright guy, very personable, but he also had a lot of bull! He'd say, 'We're gonna make it, and we're gonna make it big, don't worry.' Andy had all this talk about working, playing music, and making money. Being that we were jazz musicians, we went to rehearsals and played for free. Andy's wife bought doughnuts and gave them to us after we rehearsed. Later, Andy mentioned the gig where I'm to play the 'One O' Clock Jump' solo. Andy said, 'We're playing New Year's Eve at the Moose Hall in Bradford, Pennsylvania. We're going to drive there and put all our stuff in an open trailer.' "

Sam goes on, "It was very cold that winter, and some guys sat in the trailer with the instruments and other stuff. I did it for a while. Later, a guy from a car relieved me. We're driving to Bradford for a 9:00 pm gig when suddenly we're in the middle of a huge snowstorm. The guys in the cars couldn't see in front of them, and those in the trailer were blinded by snow. We were crawling and freezing our butts off to get to this stupid gig. I think we got there at 11:30. I've forgotten what it paid, if anything. We set up in time to play 'Auld Lang Syne,' and one band tune. We finished, packed up, and had to drive back to Buffalo. Luckily, the snow lightened up, but it was a truly horrible experience."

That was an important year for Sam Noto as one day he entered Whiteman's Song Shop on Main Street to buy a Harry James record. Sam says, "In those days music stores or record shops had listening booths where you listened to a record before buying it. If you liked it, then you paid for it. As I'm enjoying my Harry James record, two young East Side saxophone players I knew, Sam Calcaterra (Sam Cal) and Frank Busto tapped on the booth's glass window. Sam Cal opened the door and said, 'Hey, what are you doing?' "

I said, "Just listening to Harry James."

"Have you heard Bird and Diz yet?"

They took Sam to their booth and Calcaterra put on a Charlie "Bird" Parker and Dizzy Gillespie record of a tune called "Shaw 'Nuff."

After that, Sam Noto was turned around. Hearing that song was the best thing that ever happened to him. It was early in his playing career, and a real life changer in terms of the way he now began thinking about music. Florence Bloom, the wife of a local jazz DJ, was Whiteman's record clerk. She allowed young jazz musicians to spend hours listening to those fantastic records. Sam says, "Finally, after repeatedly playing and listening to 'Shaw 'Nuff,' Florence said, 'My boss is giving me the eye, you've got to get out of there.' "

In Buffalo at that time, little movie theaters that featured big bands on their stages were everywhere. Musically, much was happening here. Sam Noto played in one of those theaters with the Andy James Band. Sam says, "I forget the name, it was on Grant and Ferry. Oh yeah—the Victoria. I think it's now a supermarket or something. My brother Bill had formed a big band, Gabriel Norton and his Orchestra, that played there. I was in that band. It makes me laugh; Bill kept his initials but changed his last name. At that time I hung out with Frank Picone, a good trumpet player my age. We played a Be-Bop concert in one of those theaters."

In 1946, Sam was entering his junior year at Burgard High School. He hadn't yet quit and was still in the school band. In those days many Buffalo musicians, young and old, hung out drinking coffee at the Waldorf, a restaurant on Court and Franklin Streets. Al Bonati, a trumpet player who was an older brother of Sam's good friend, alto man Joe (Mouse) Bonati, saw Sam there. He told Sam he was going on the road down South with the Allen Craig Band, and said, "They need another trumpet player, do you want the gig?" Sam says, "I didn't hesitate for a second. Al said, 'It's a commercial band and it pays sixty dollars a week.' "

Sixteen-year-old Sam, who knew that the minimum wage was forty cents an hour, immediately agreed to go. Al Bonati called Pops, Allen Craig's road manager to say, "I have the other trumpet man."

Pops said, "Okay, you know where to meet us in Richmond, Virginia; bring him with you."

Sam Noto quit school and told his parents he was going on the road to play in a band down South.

Sam says, "My mother started to cry. My father said, 'what can we do, let him go.' "

ON THAT LONG, LONG LONESOME ROAD

At the New York Central Terminal on Paderewski Drive, Sam and Al boarded a train to Richmond, Virginia. Upon arriving, they went to their assigned hotel. When Sam was alone in his room he started crying. He missed his parents and his friends in Buffalo. But there he was, young and traveling. Sam says, "I didn't know what the hell I was doing, but I was doing it—and doing it as a member of Allen Craig's Orchestra. I didn't know then that these kinds of bands were called territory bands, or Mickey Mouse bands. We played country clubs and dances in Georgia, Alabama—throughout the South. One morning in Florida we're having breakfast in our hotel, and we see Pops, who said, 'Allen Craig and the female vocalist absconded with the band's entire payroll.'

"Me and Al Bonati were stranded. Pops told us he talked to a guy near Tampa who would hire the band for a week."

From that gig Al and Sam earned enough to bus it back home.

That was Sam's first real road experience other than the Andy James Moose Hall fiasco. It, too, was dreadful. In many of Sam's stories, depression and regrets arrive at various times. He often wondered if he, so young, was doing the right thing. "A lot of bad stuff happens when you're coming up and you want to play and suddenly you realize everyone is not honest."

The next couple of years in Sam's life were spent hanging out in Buffalo going to jam sessions, sitting in, and honing his skills at Banny's on Niagara Street and other spots. Sunday afternoons were spent on Broadway and Michigan jamming at the Colored Musicians Local. He was learning more and more: tunes, scales, and chord changes that he'd apply to his playing style, etc. He was happy to be home and played any gig he could get, such as dances and casuals. He joined a popular West Seneca area orchestra led by pianist Freddie Reeb. Sam says, "Freddie had a drummer, Cliff Wahl, with great chops who later became an ordained minister. It was a fairly good dance band. The bass player was Tibby Tiberio, and on trumpet with me were Frank Picone and Danny Lampone. The sax section had Joe Campagna, Tony Sorrento, Billy Licata, and some East Side guys. Every Friday night we played at St. Theresa's Parish Hall in South Buffalo, and we earned six dollars apiece."

Those earnings disappeared at the Duquesne Pool Hall and Bowling Lanes on Washington Street where everyone went after the gig to bowl, shoot pool, and play pinball machines, and they loved every minute of it.

Freddie Reeb's band played other gigs. As such, Sam had money in his pocket. He was living with his parents and had few responsibilities. It was soon 1950, and while Sam was on Main Street jamming at Bafo's, Clyde McCoy and his orchestra were in town playing at a nearby theater. McCoy was immortalized for his best-selling recording of "Sugar Blues." Andy Khan, a trumpet player from Pittsburgh who Sam didn't know, and who was in McCoy's orchestra, was also jamming at Bafo's. When Danny heard Sam he told him he (Danny) had given McCoy two weeks-notice and would Sam replace him? Sam said, "I'd love that."

An audition with McCoy's road manager was set up. Danny Khan worked his two weeks, Sam was hired, and was told to meet McCoy's band in Cleveland, Ohio, at such and such a place and on such and such a date.

On the day Sam was to join McCoy, he and his brother Bill, both New York Yankees fans, drove to Cleveland to see the Yankees play the Indians. Sam says, "Oh man, I got to see all those great stars. Joe DiMaggio, close to retirement left in the seventh inning. His replacement was a young Yankee named Mickey Mantle. Gil McDougal played third base, Phil Rizzuto was at shortstop, Yogi Berra was the catcher, Eddie Lopat pitched, and the Yankees won eight to zero."

After the game, Sam Noto joined the big name band of Clyde McCoy to play third trumpet. It was an opening night somewhere in Cleveland featuring McCoy, an obscure comic, and the headliner, Miss Patti Page, The Singing Rage. Sam said, "We open playing three or four tunes, then the comic, then Clyde does his celebrated version of 'Sugar Blues,' everyone goes nuts, and then comes an intermission."

It was then that Sam knew why Danny Kahn had left the band. Playing third meant you had little to do. There were no solos. It was all Clyde McCoy. Sam took his fate in stride and toured with the band playing the southern dates featuring Patti Page.

Trombonists Jack Hitchcock and Jack Harmon from Long Island were in the band. After Sam heard them play jazz-oriented riffs, he befriended them. McCoy was a strict disciplinarian. He made periodic announcements, "In my band no drinking or drugs are tolerated." One night, before a gig in a Galveston, Texas hotel ballroom, Sam, Hitchcock, and Harmon were there to dine. "The Jacks," who were older than Sam, ordered martinis before dinner. Sam had water with his meal. Sam says, "At that moment, Clyde McCoy enters. He sees 'the Jacks' drinking and fires them on the spot. He fired the two best players in the band! He looked at me, saw I was drinking water, and said nothing."

The band played that night. After which "the Jacks," who passionately hated McCoy and the redundancy of "Sugar Blues," told Sam they were glad to be fired. They, like Sam, were jazz players and hearing McCoy's "corn" was an affront.

The playlist had one trumpet solo that wasn't McCoy's. It was on a foreign tune called "Bahia," and it was in the second trumpet book played by Bob Ariel. When Patti Page's tour ended, the band played dances, etc. Ariel, who was having "chops trouble," turned to Sam and asked, "Would you play the 'Bahia' solo?"

Sam, apprehensive, asked, "What would Clyde say?"

"Sam, just play what's on the paper."

Sam agreed.

Sam told me, "Bahia had a Latin flavor. It began with four measures of trumpet melody, the drummer gives a burst, and the band swings. I ignored the written solo and played a jazz version. Clyde McCoy leans over and starts waving, flailing his arms, saying no, no, no, and while people were dancing he orders the band to stop."

The players loved Sam's solo, especially "the Jacks." At intermission Clyde McCoy approached Sam and said, "I should fire you!"

Sam, astonished, said, "Why? I was helping Bob. He's having problems with his chops."

Clyde said, "You're not supposed to play that stuff with those high notes you were doing. You belong in a band like Stan Kenton's."

Sam said, "That's the way I felt the solo."

"That's too bad," said McCoy. "I take the solos in this band."

Sam said, "You? If you took that mute from your horn you'd hear what you really sound like, and that's garbage! Your sound is the worst. It's like you-know-what, and you don't have to fire me; I quit!"

Sam didn't know quitting meant he must pay his own way home. Had he waited to be fired McCoy would've had to pay his return fare, but Sam was impetuous. Upon arriving in Buffalo, he learned that he had been drafted into the United States Army. By then his parents had moved to the Upper West Side on Barton Street near the Mt. Major Hall. One Saturday night Sam heard a live band playing there. He entered the hall and saw a wedding reception in progress. Danny Lampone, the band's trumpet player, glad to see Sam, asked about the McCoy debacle that every musician in town was privy to. Sam told him the story. Danny laughed, and asked Sam, "What are you doing tomorrow night?"

"Not much, why?"

Danny said he was taking a date to Crystal Beach (in nearby Canada) to hear Jimmy Dorsey's Orchestra and offered to get Sam a blind date, to which Sam responded, "I don't go with blind dates." Danny insisted, saying, "No, no, she's a nice girl."

Sam, with nothing to do, said okay. The next day Danny and his girl picked up Sam and drove to the home of Sam's blind date; the young, lovely Arleen Christian. The couples drove to Canada, where they had a good time. Sam told Arleen he wasn't a good dancer but would give the slow stuff a try. Returning, Arleen was humming a solo from a Charlie Parker record. Sam asked, "What's that you're humming?"

She said, "Oh, you wouldn't know."

Sam said," What do you mean I wouldn't know? That sounds like something Charlie Parker would play."

"Yes, it is! I have his records."

Sam couldn't believe it. "No kidding, that's unbelievable!"

Back in Buffalo they visited the Anchor Bar for outstanding Italian food and to hear Joe Bonati who was playing there, and there the night ended.

THE ARMY AND ON THE ROAD AGAIN

By autumn, Sam Noto was in Fort Dix, New Jersey, a member of the United States Army. Sam told me, "As tough and thick-skinned as I'm alleged to be, the incident with Clyde McCoy was discouraging. I was drained emotionally, and I didn't know what to do. Now I'm a soldier while I'm passionately involved with Arleen Christian who I missed terribly. I was unhappy. My thought process was scattered and owing to army life I couldn't think properly."

Sam Noto was politically oblivious. He knew American forces were fighting an undeclared war in North Korea, but he was into his music, not Korea. He knew nothing about war, but he knew that if it came to our shores he'd fight for his country, his family, and his friends. Though unable to assimilate, he did manage to audition for the army band. From his earlier road experience, sight reading music was easy. He didn't have his trumpet with him, only a mouthpiece, so the army supplied him one. At the audition he played any and all music put in front of him. Everyone said, "Great, great. After basic training, consider yourself a member of the army band."

Before basic training Sam went to a few rehearsals and heard some good army musicians. He learned more about chords and much about the music he was deeply into from a piano player who had worked with Stan Getz and whose name he can't recall. Because the incorrigible Sam Noto never finished basic training, he wasn't accepted in the army band.

Sam says, "It was a terrible experience. I was discharged from the United States Army 'At the Convenience of the Government.' It wasn't a dishonorable discharge. Then, the U.S. Government had what was an educational benefit for veterans who served over ninety days. They got rid of me before the ninety days expired."

The U.S. Government, upon freeing itself of Sam Noto, wasn't financially obligated to provide future education should civilian Noto decide to seek it. Now home, he was cynical, confused, and trying to develop the music part of his life. He couldn't find a gig, and he convinced himself that no one cared for his trumpet playing. He also thought that if he was good at that, then other parts of his life—like making a living—would take care of itself. Wrong, wrong again!

Sam says, "What's the point? I thought of quitting music and finding a day job." As his relationship with Arleen intensified, a call came from a Town Casino trombonist named Angelo Callea who knew of Sam's ability. Callea told Sam that he had implored Moe Balsom, the Towne Casino bandleader, to hire him as his third trumpeter to complement Vince Impellitier and Pete Crino. So, when Casino headliners called for more musicians, Moe Balsom would hire Sam.

"That was a good thing," says Sam, "because assuming I couldn't find a day gig, the Towne Casino on Main Street was better in terms of money, and I was playing there sporadically."

The wheels were in motion. Sam began subbing at the Palace Burlesk. "That gig paid better than any day job would," says Sam, "and with no experience with day gigs, the Palace was the real deal for a young, unmarried man living with his parents." Still, Sam wanted to earn more money, knowing that most people strive for that to live better. (For the record, burlesque is the correct spelling of the word. Knowing that the proper spelling would take additional lightbulbs on the marquee, proprietor Dewey Michaels chose to spell it burlesk.)

Sam was seeing Arleen more and was made aware of its seriousness when she announced that she was pregnant. Sam, still trying to do what he knew, jammed at sessions in Bafo's. One night, Vinnie Tano, a trumpet player from Philadelphia in town with Dean Hudson's band, was at Bafo's. Lionel Hampton's band was there, and its players heard Vinnie and convinced Hampton to hire him. Vinnie heard Sam, and asked Sam to take his former place in Dean Hudson's band. Sam, doing what he called "odds and ends" in Buffalo, was elated and said yes. But the destructive drawback to his departure was his involvement with the increasingly pregnant Arleen.

That aside, Sam left town the next day with Dean Hudson's band, comfortable knowing that a Buffalo friend, trumpet man Chuck San Filippo, was a bandmate. Dean Hudson was also a trumpet player, and he led this very good commercial band with its customary amounts of brass, reed, and percussion players. Most of their work was in the elite part of the South: U.S. military officers' clubs, various army bases, golf clubs, etc. Sam smiles and says, "Everyone loved Dean Hudson. He was a real personable guy, you couldn't help loving him. He was straight on all the time. Dean had another "book" (arrangements), it was almost like a jazz book with one trumpet and five saxophones. I never got to play it. I heard about it, but I only played the commercial arrangements. We played all the popular songs of the day, and 30s and 40s. I was with Dean off and on for a couple of years."

Meanwhile in Buffalo, Arleen's parents, Arthur and the former Irene Powers, were devastated about Arleen's condition. They called Sam a few times while he was on the road. Sam says, "How they had the number to call or knew where I was remains a mystery to this day. The question was always the same, 'What are you doing about the situation?' "

Sam was at his wit's end, going crazy about something he partially created, and wishing he never did. The proverbial confusion that haunted him earlier was surfacing at a rapid pace. He was distracted and consumed with guilt about Arleen Christian's circumstances.

THE FAMILIAR STRAIN FROM HERNIA AND THE CALL

One night while on a Hudson gig Sam, playing with considerable force, suffered a hernia. Sam says, "I felt the thing pop out. I left the band and went home for an operation and couldn't play for ten weeks. Nothing. I couldn't practice, not for a minute, for fear of opening the stitches. My days were spent watching TV, and again wondering, perusing the rest of my life."

To make matters worse, his parents had to help him maneuver the stairs—up or down. He was stranded again, this time for ten weeks, but unlike as in Florida, he was at home. When the recuperation period ended, he began visiting Bafo's. Sam told me, "That was about 1952. You go where the people you know are, where you're known, you know, like the TV show Cheers. You go where people know your name. I saw lots of guys, old friends; Callea, Frank Primerano, Frank Picone, and others. I hung out and pretty soon I started playing again. I went to jam sessions, there were many here, and I was getting back into my music. Frank Picone and I would play high notes all day, emulating Maynard Ferguson's stratospheric style. One day I'm home practicing and the phone rings. I picked it up, said 'hello,' and a man's voice says, 'Is this Sam Noto?'

"I said, 'Yes,' and the man said, 'This is Stan Kenton.'" Sam was flustered and hung up.

Sam went on, "I thought it was Callea or Picone putting me on and playing with my head." He went on practicing. The phone rang again. The same voice said, "Sam Noto?"

Sam said, "Suddenly I recognized the voice. This was authentic. If you know that era, Stan Kenton introduced Maynard Ferguson, Buddy Childers, Conte Candoli and Richie Kamuca, and others before they soloed. Guys on the band were hot, that whole band was hot."

Stan Kenton said, "I need a couple of trumpet players tonight for a gig in Buffalo. Joe Gustaferro at the musician's union told me to call you because you've got high note chops that are needed to replace Conte Candoli in my band. Can you do the gig tonight at Shea's Great Lakes Theatre?"

Sam jubilantly agreed, and Kenton told him to be at the Pearl Street door of the theatre at 6:00 pm to run over the music with Buddy Childers, the first trumpet player.

How well Sam Noto remembers the circumstances that led to him getting in the band! He told me, "Conte Candoli and his then pregnant wife were on a bus that crashed somewhere in Pennsylvania. Conti was hurt, and his wife cracked something in her spine. It was a bad thing. George Morley, Kenton's road manager who was also on the bus, flew out the windshield. He was found on the side of the road with his neck wide open, but he lived.

"I arrived at the theatre at about twenty minutes to six to warm up. At the stage door a man said, 'Can I help you?' "

Sam told him what he was there for and the man directed him to the boiler room, where he said the rehearsal was to be. Sam found the room empty. All the stands were set up with music. "I took out my horn and began warming up. As I did, Georgie Holt, the other trumpet player hired for the gig, arrived. George was a good musician from the colored local and was a friend of mine. Some band guys started trickling in, as did Buddy Childers. George and I didn't rehearse the whole show, but Buddy took us through the more difficult stuff so we didn't bust our chops before the gig. He did a wonderful job. He told us where the high parts were and what we should be doing, and George and I did a good job of understanding him. We still had a few minutes before show time, so I went upstairs and had a cup of coffee. Before the concert began the curtain was kept closed, and all the musicians were behind their stands. When the curtain opened, Stan Kenton came out to loud applause. He waved to George and me, the new guys. Then he looked at drummer Stan Levy and nodded his head vigorously as Levy started rolling his drumsticks on the cymbals to deafening pitch, and the band started playing 'Artistry in Rhythm.' Buddy Childers played a high G for four bars while the reeds and trombones played their parts. The hairs on the back of my neck started standing up because, you know, you've heard this stuff on records and on the radio, and now you're in the same band playing it!

"The concert went well. At intermission Stan came over and spoke to George and me. Then he asked Buddy how we were doing. Buddy said, 'They're doing great, very well, they're reading the charts okay, everything's fine.' "

Sam Noto had had years of experience playing and reading big band charts with Allen Craig, Clyde McCoy, and Dean Hudson. When the concert ended, Kenton received a phone call from Conte Candoli who informed him that he wasn't returning to the band. He had busted his chops in the accident, and his pregnant wife had problems. Stan Kenton told Sam, "Conte may be back, I don't really know. Would you like to come on the road for a few weeks?"

Sam quickly agreed, and Kenton said, "Good! The bus leaves at 8:00 am tomorrow morning from the Touraine Hotel on Delaware Avenue. Can you meet us there?"

That's how that momentous night in 1952 ended. Sam later learned that Arleen had been in the audience. He says, "When the curtain opened and Arleen saw me in the trumpet section, she said she whispered, 'Whoa, okay, it looks like he's going to be gone for a while.' "

JOINING STAN KENTON'S BAND

Sam says, "After the concert I was ecstatic. I went home and started packing. My parents saw me. They said, 'Where are you going?'

"I said, 'I'm going on the road with the Stan Kenton Orchestra.' My father looked sad, and my mother cried. She was always crying. They wouldn't have known Stan Kenton from a dish of tripe. I said, 'Ma, Pa, this is a very famous band, not like the others, and it's a great opportunity for me.' My father said I could go. They wished me luck. What else could they do? I'd been on the road before so that announcement wasn't too hard to make."

With his horn and his packed bag in hand, Sam Noto left for the Hotel Touraine and arrived early. The band bus was in front with the motor running. Sam boarded the bus, but it was empty except for the driver. Sam put his trumpet and bag in an upper compartment and sat in a seat. As he did, Sal Salvador, Kenton's guitarist, got on the bus and sat next to Sam. He said, "You're one of the trumpet players from last night."

Sam and Sal had that Italian thing going. They became fast friends talking about the road, jazz, the band, and music in general. Sal Salvador was pleasant and made Sam comfortable. Sam, meanwhile, watched in amazement as drummer Stan Levy, trombonist Frank Rosolino, and other Kenton stars entered the bus.

Sam told me, "Suddenly, Zoot Sims, who with Stan Getz years ago had been on Woody Herman's classic recording Four Brothers, is on the bus. Zoot saw me sitting next to Sal and stared at me with a look indicative of a man hung-over, and continued to do so. I was comfortable with Sal, but Zoot changed that. Finally, an angry Zoot said, 'Aaaarrrhhh, you're in my seat, man!' I panicked and apologized profusely, 'I'm sorry, I'm sorry! I didn't know!' I got up, and Zoot the intimidator sat in his assigned seat. Sal Salvador offered to help me find a new one. I saw an empty one in the back and thanked Sal and left to occupy what would be my home and my bed for the next two weeks."

Soon, other stars including Stan Kenton were on the bus and it drove away. An awe-struck Sam Noto had no idea where it was going or where it would take him. Ultimately, it arrived in some small town where the band repeated what they had played in Buffalo. Sam says, "We were on the road a couple of weeks. One night we're in Chicago playing a concert at the Opera House. At intermission I went out the back door. On the street I saw Zoot Sims talking to someone. I went back in. Soon after, I saw Zoot enter. He had 'pin eyes.' He leaned against a wall, struck a match, and tried to light a cigarette, but instead burned his fingers. He was wiped out, drugged. He couldn't lift his arm to light the cigarette and kept burning his fingers. He tried several times; same thing. I couldn't watch anymore. I grabbed his arm and raised it so the lit match would light the cigarette. The grouchy son-of-a-bitch was grateful, but he was bugged at the same time. He looked at me, gave me one of his big, classic aaaarrrhhhhhs, and walked away. I never forgot that night. It was sad and yet, funny."

The next day Stan Kenton announced to all, "We're going to Texas for a big concert tour with some heavy stars; Charlie Parker and Dizzy Gillespie for openers, and many, many other greats. We're meeting in Houston and we'll rehearse there."

Sam remembers the event. It was called "The Festival of Modern Jazz Tour." The youthful and dedicated Sam Noto, who had experienced sporadic feelings of inadequacy while back in Buffalo, was now electrified, filled with untold confidence. Playing with the Stan Kenton Orchestra, seeing and hearing Charlie "Bird" Parker and Dizzy in person, and in front of a band that he, himself was in, and hearing what he had heard in Whiteman's Song Shop all those years ago made him ecstatic. It was an incredible dream, a thrilling and memorable event of his burgeoning life. For three months Sam Noto was on the same stage playing with and listening to the genius of jazz giants Charlie "Bird" Parker and Dizzy Gillespie.

Three busloads of musicians traveling at night were on that tour, including The Art Tatum Trio, and groups led by Shelly Manne, Shorty Rogers, Charlie Ventura, and Stan Getz. One night, Sam and alto man Charlie Mariano, who was Sam's roommate and a disciple of Bird, were on the band bus. They were beat and dying to sleep in a real bed. Finally, when the bus stopped and they were leaving, Bird approached them to ask if they would like to see a movie with him. Not wanting to disappoint him, they agreed.

According to Sam, "We entered the theater, bought popcorn, and sat. A Pink Panther cartoon came on, and as it progressed all you heard throughout the theater was Bird's loud laughter. When the feature began, all you heard was Bird's snoring. He was totally out of it. Mariano and I left him there and split to find a hotel, a place to sleep."

At that time Sam played fourth and fifth trumpet parts in Kenton's band and never soloed. Later in the tour Buddy Childers would slip him an occasional lead part that wasn't exorbitant, and it gave Sam some exposure. Sam recalls early on when the Kenton band was in Detroit playing opposite Duke Ellington's. "At intermission, me and Frank Rosolino were outside in an alley smoking a joint. Stan came out. It was dark, but he saw us and walked away. Kenton liked people. He liked me, and he liked Rosolino, but after the concert he fired us. The next morning everyone boarded the bus. The driver is counting heads. Stan stood, arms up, faced the band and tells the bus driver, 'Don't go yet. I want to talk to the band. Last night I saw something, and I fired two guys. I'm sure you all know who they are. I don't like any marijuana smoking on this band or any kind of drugs, but I'm giving them a second chance.' "

Sam recalls, "At the time I was only a section player. If I were doing a joint with someone else in that alley I'd be gone. But I was with Frank Rosolino, a featured player."

Wherever the band was, Sam scoured the landscape looking for clubs in which to "sit in" as he did in Buffalo. Sam says, "We were in Cincinnati, Ohio, and a great trumpet player, Bill Berry, was in some club playing with Dee Felice, a local drummer. I heard about it. After a concert I went there and asked if I could sit in. They said, 'Yeah, man, come on up.' I played a set and had a great time. I didn't know Stan Kenton was in the audience. When I got off the stand he called me over to where he was sitting. 'I didn't know you were a jazz player,' he said. I said, 'I don't go around telling people I play jazz.' Kenton said, 'Well, man, we've got to do something about that; maybe I'll give you a solo here and there, huh? Would you like that?' I said, 'I'd love it.' Kenton asked me to sit and said, 'If you want to stay on the band you can. Conte Candoli is in Los Angeles and isn't coming back.' "

At that moment an excited Sam Noto was a permanent member of Stan Kenton's Orchestra. Rooming with the knowledgeable Charlie Mariano he learned more about music, chords, and various progressions. Mariano explained how chords, altered chords, and key progressions worked. He taught Sam everything he wanted to know. In their hotel room Sam muted his trumpet, and with his new-found knowledge he explored what to do when given the chance to solo.

On the "Festival of Modern Jazz" tour, Sam became friends with Dizzy. Wherever Dizzy was, Sam was near him. He always wanted to hear what Dizzy was talking about, what he was saying. Sam says, "As to Bird? I became close to him as well. When he felt good, like when he wasn't strung out on heroin, Bird was like Dizzy, friendly, like that time at the movies."

There was a lot of gambling on that tour, day and night; dice, poker, all kinds of stuff. Those sessions on the bus and in the dressing rooms were pretty brutal, out of hand. One night, Bird was playing dice and losing all his money, and he was angry. Sam says, "I wasn't doing so good either. I had my last twenty dollars in my hand. Dizzy had the dice and he was doing okay. Bird told Dizzy, 'I'll bet twenty dollars you don't make your point.' Bird didn't put any money on the floor. Dizzy looked at Bird and said 'Bird, I don't see any bread down there.' Bird saw the twenty in my hand and said, 'Sam, give me that twenty.' I said I couldn't—I was losing too—and Bird kept insisting and I kept refusing. Bird cursed me out and stormed from the room."

On another night, Sam had one hundred dollars in his pocket and bet it all in a no-limit poker game. With four-of-a-kind he won a Roloflex camera from Buddy Childers. Sam tells it this way. "Buddy called me, and I said, 'Well, man, you've got to put up the money.' Buddy reached into a bag under his seat and pulled out a Roloflex camera and said, 'Would this cover it?' I said, 'Yeah, of course,' and Buddy put the camera on the table. Then he showed his cards: a full house, but it couldn't beat my four-of-a-kind! Buddy went ballistic. I, with my new-found possession, was taking pictures of all the jazz greats around me.

"I took black and white still pictures of Bird standing and playing next to a prop. Before I knew it, Danny Ebersole, a guy I knew in New York, put the pictures I took in a book. I don't know how that happened. Then Ebersole put out a poster of one of my Bird stills and was selling it. I was bugged about that. I don't know how he got them, but he did."

Sam has incredible memories about that Festival tour and the greats he met, and with whom he played. One night the band was in a club and Stan Kenton was sitting with a distinguished looking gentleman. Kenton, with a hand gesture, invited Sam to his table and introduced him to Igor Stravinsky, whose music Sam was very much into. Sam was stunned, speechless, and thrilled beyond words. Sam told Stravinsky how much he loved "Ebony Concerto," a stunning work Stravinsky wrote in 1946 for Woody Herman's orchestra.

Sam says, "In December when the tour ended, Kenton said they were going to LA to record two albums of arrangements by tenor man Bill Holman and trombonist Bill Russo." Sam Noto soloed on those albums, and though he wasn't happy with his playing, everyone around him liked what he did. With his new-found recording recognition and ample money, that session was a good thing. Later the band was told they'd be off and would start up again in in March 1954.

I'LL BE HOME FOR CHRISTMAS

Sam flew to Buffalo, arriving just before Christmas. It was great being with family, sitting around and talking with Arleen. Financially it was rough, but he subbed at the Towne Casino and at the Palace Burlesk, scratching out a living while waiting to hear from his leader.

The call from Kenton came as expected in March 1954, and the band toured again. This time they were alone, except for five months of shows with Tony Bennett, after which they disbanded. Sam came home again, and on August 28, 1954, he married Arleen Christian, the mother of his first son, the now two-year-old Michael Noto. Sam waited for Stan to reorganize, knowing that he would be called. But that call didn't come.

Sam, Arlene, and Michael had recently moved from Arleen's parents' home to a flat on West Delevan Avenue near Grant Street, and it didn't have a telephone. Finally, in January 1955 a clerk who worked at the nearby corner drugstore and who knew Sam told him that Stan Kenton had called their place looking for him. The pharmacist let him make a collect call to Stan Kenton. They spoke, and Sam was back on the road. That 1955 band with lead trumpeter Al Porcino, Ed Leddy, Charlie Mariano, and Carl Fontana was the band that recorded the famous Chicago Contemporary Concepts album. They were on the road doing one-nighters for nine months. They played Birdland in New York, and a week at the Blue Note in Chicago. Unlike the earlier tour with

Dizzy and Bird, this wasn't as much fun, but it was a good band with great players.

Before long, the band was in Los Angeles, and Al Porcino insisted—demanded that everyone in the section play trumpets made by Eldon Benge. Porcino said that in order to get the right sound you had to play a Benge. But before that could happen, Porcino went to New York for something and Ed Leddy became Kenton's first trumpet player. Leddy and Sam were inquisitive and sought out Eldon Benge, the legendary trumpet player, who lived and built his trumpets in nearby Burbank. They found him at his home at 1122 West Burbank Boulevard. He was maybe sixty, seventy years old, and walked bent over as if crippled. Sam and Ed learned that Eldon Benge suffered from severe arthritis and was in constant pain. While they were in Mr. Benge's back yard smoking a joint, Mr. Benge exited the house with a quantity of booze and asked them what they were up to. Sam told me, "We told him, and Eldon Benge starts smoking weed; first time in his life. Soon Eldon said, 'My pain is disappearing.' " Sam said, "Really? Keep smoking, man."

Sam went on, "The three of us went in the house. Ed and I were eating and drinking, and Eldon Benge disappeared. Soon he returned with two beautiful horns and he is STONED! Mr. Benge says, 'Play something for me.' " Sam says, "With Mr. Benge's handmade trumpets Ed and I played Bill Holman's chart on 'Stomping at the Savoy.' Eldon Benge says, 'Good one, good one, I love it. I love it!' Suddenly the cops are there saying that it was eleven thirty and the neighbors were complaining. That was an exciting night."

In 1955, while in Buffalo on a break from Kenton, Sam received a phone call from one of the Latona brothers, the new owners of the Copa Casino, a Main Street jazz club that featured big name artists. He said, "Sam, can you put a band together for two weeks to back up a girl singer? You don't have to play your trumpet for her, just do a couple of tunes with your group, announce her, bring her on, leave the stand, and your guys accompany her." Sam agreed and hired Bill Rasey, who could play for singers, and Frank Primerano on bass. Sam says, "I heard Mel Lewis, the drummer who had just left Ray Anthony's band, was in town so I called his home. Mel's mother answers the phone, and we have this conversation.

"Hello, this is Sam Noto; is Mel there?"

"Who's calling?"

"Sam Noto."

"Who?"

"Sam Noto."

"Well, what's it about?"

"Is he there or not?"

"I want to know what it's about."

"I have a two week job at Latona's and I need to know if he wants to play drums."

"How much does it pay?"

"It pays scale."

"I'm going to give him a message. You're sure it's for scale?"

"Yes! It pays scale."

Mel's mother hangs up on Sam. Sam starts perusing the phone book for drummers. The phone rings.

"Sam, it's Mel Lewis. What's going on, man? You got a gig for me?"

"Yeah."

"You know I'm leaving to join Stan Kenton"

"So am I."

Mel said, "You know, I could use a gig before I go. Is it still open?"

"Yeah, and it pays scale."

"Yeah, I know."

They did the gig. For two weeks Sam played two tunes, introduced the singer whose name he has now forgotten, and then flew to Los Angeles with Mel.

Before long Al Porcino returned to the band and was playing lead. Sam was doing quite a bit of soloing, but for whatever reason, Al didn't like Sam. He gave Sam's solos to Stu Williamson. That frustrated Sam. He tried repeatedly to quit the band, but Stan wouldn't have any of that. Some time passed. In New York, the band was busing it to a gig. When they arrived, Sam told Stan, "I won't be here tomorrow night." Kenton said, "Sam, don't start with that again, okay?" Sam says, "At the hotel I packed my bag, went to the Greyhound station on Eighth Avenue and 51st, and hopped a bus to Buffalo."

Just like that he quit on the spot, knowing Kenton could, if he so chose, bring him up on charges with the Musicians Union. Sam didn't care. He regretted the situation that caused his unorthodox departure. He knew he'd miss Charlie Mariano. They were great friends, great musicians, and were inseparable. Mariano's guidance had helped make Sam the world class trumpet player he would become. In addition to Porcino's antics, Sam was becoming increasingly disenchanted with traveling. The vagabond life of a big band musician was losing its veneer, a veneer once sought by young musicians.

THE PALACE AND SHUFFLE OFF TO EUROPE

Back home, Sam replaced Casey Ventura in the Palace Burlesk band to become its permanent trumpeter. Piano man Roy Ricotta was the leader, Sam Sokoloff, Mel Lewis's father, played drums, and Bill Wullin played saxophone. For obvious reasons, owing to his impetuous New York exodus, Sam didn't expect to return to Kenton. Luckily, the Palace's twenty-nine weekly shows were his. There were four shows daily, five on Saturday, plus a midnight show seven days, seven nights. They played a show, then came a movie, another show, another movie, and coming attractions. As such, Sam knew the extensive time he'd spend in the pit would become his life. He and the others arrived at eleven in the morning and were there till eleven thirty in the evening, with two hours off for dinner. Arleen was upset because he left in the morning, came home for dinner, and left again, and when he returned at night she'd be sleeping.

Between shows Sam and his musical pals had pasta at Henry's Café next door, or played horseshoes for beer at Danny Rinaldo's, a nearby saloon. By the time the fourth show ended they were wacked out.

In February 1956, after doing that routine for some time, Sam received a surprise phone call from Stan Kenton. After polite greetings, Sam apologized to Kenton for leaving as he did in New York City. He asked Kenton why he wasn't reported to the union. Kenton said, "I wouldn't do that to you, Sam. I thought we'd work it out." Kenton paused and said, "Sam, we're going to Europe and I want you in the band."

Sam told Kenton, "I'm not interested. I can't sit next to Al Porcino."

"No, Sam," said Kenton, "he isn't in the band. Ed Leddy is playing first trumpet. You, Vinnie Tano, Lee Katzman, and another hire are it. Can you fly to California to meet us?" Sam was elated and agreed. Kenton said, "We're doing one-nighters from LA to New York. Then we sail to Cherbourg, France on the Queen Elizabeth. You can bring your wife. I'll pay her traveling expenses and you can pay for your room and food." Sam went to California, did the one-nighters, and when the band arrived in New York City he left for Buffalo to get Arleen.

The Palace Burlesk, an integral part of Sam Noto's life in Buffalo, was now obscured. With Stan Kenton's orchestra Sam played in Europe and in England. Then, in 1956, the English and American musicians' unions conflicted. Their bands weren't allowed here and ours weren't allowed there. Somehow it was agreed that Kenton could play in England for five weeks, and the English band of Ted Heath could play here for five weeks. Sam and Arleen boarded the Queen Elizabeth, a crossing that took four or five days. It was March, and the North Atlantic was rough. A walk to the dining area wasn't safe. Ropes were set up for people to hang on to. Arleen Noto had no problem with food, but Sam, nauseous from a weather-related upset stomach, nibbled on dinner rolls. Preparing for their forthcoming concerts, the band rehearsed a few times in the hold of the ship. One day, the crew and workers were invited to attend a rehearsal. Sam told me, "Weather-wise it was uncomfortable, and as we played our music stands moved from us. Mel Lewis's drums sneaked from him each time the ship tilted, but after that first day it was fun, like a vacation. The drinks were twelve cents and the food was included in the price of the fare."

The ship docked in France. Before going to England, Sam and Arleen did the tourist thing and bought a huge bottle of cognac for ten dollars. After an hour or two they returned to the ship and it crossed the channel to England.

Sam says, "On our first night in England a large party ensued in a hotel ballroom; a buffet with great food, booze, beer, and wine was enjoyed as Ted Heath's band entertained. Kenton did two two-hour concerts a day. It wasn't much fun. In addition to bad weather there wasn't any central heating in our hotel room, and shillings were needed for the heater. In the middle of the night the shilling time would expire, and you'd freeze your you-know-what off. It was a horrible situation. The hotel maid would enter the room with hot water bottles and put them at our feet while we were in bed. No matter what you were doing, they'd just walk in. Then you'd go to the front desk for more shillings for the heater and they're out of shillings. The food? Horrible! All boiled stuff. They had tongue sandwiches. That whole experience was a lot of work, a lot of work."

When Kenton finished that tour, which included the Royal Albert Hall and Brisbane, the band went to Scotland and Wales. Sam recalls, "Those five weeks were tedious; full of work and little time for the musicians to do anything but play. The morning was breakfast, then perform a two o'clock show, finish at four, have dinner somewhere and then prepare for the eight o'clock show. After that it was time for bed."

Soon the band flew to Oslo for four weeks. Ed Leddy was ill on the plane that would take them to their first gig on the Continent. Sam says, "I saw that Ed didn't look well, that he seemed confused. I spoke to him and I touched him. He was burning up. I informed the stewardess, and Kenton informed the captain."

When the plane landed in Oslo an ambulance took Ed Leddy to a hospital. When Sam learned that Ed had double pneumonia, he recalled a night in England when Ed, after hitting a high note, winced and grabbed his neck. Sam had seen that Ed was in pain.

With Leddy hospitalized, Stan Kenton approached Sam to ask, "Sam, what will we do with only four trumpets?" Sam suggested calling New York to fly someone in. Kenton said, "No, you're playing first trumpet."

Sam was shocked. "What?? Oh no man, you're kidding."

Kenton said, "No, that's the way it's going to be. You play first, and you give away stuff that the others can handle, and you can solo as often as you want, don't you worry about that." Sam told Kenton he'd do it as long as Kenton paid Leddy while he was hospitalized. Kenton said it was already happening.

At that moment, Sam Noto, Stan Kenton's new lead trumpeter, joined an extraordinary cast of players from bygone years: the aforementioned Buddy Childers, Maynard Ferguson, Conrad Gozzo, Pete Candoli, Ray Wetzel, John Howell, Al Porcino, Chuck Schmidt, Bill Chase, and Marvin Stamm for openers. Sam had chops. He could hit double high notes when needed. The band loved his lead work and, as Sam says, "They were freaking out." He was getting into it and having fun. He had the strength, he was an enormously creative and dynamic twenty-six-year-old on his way to becoming a jazz trumpet genius. He and the trumpet men rehearsed what they had played and what they knew, but now they were only four. They checked out the different notes on their new assignments. Sam was on top with all the high notes. They did it. All the playing in Europe paid off. The band was fantastic. They did two shows a day and traveled from country to country. Sam says, "I was amazed at Europe's geography. The countries were close together, like states. The band was on a train to Germany that included a huge, incredible buffet. Europe was fantastic!"

It was a tour most people of Sam and Arleen's economic strata couldn't afford at any time. The band arrived in Paris where four days of gigs were planned, and they were sensational, as was the response. Sam enjoyed his new lead role and became more and more confident. Stan Kenton saw something in Sam Noto; he knew Sam was special, and he loved his playing. So did the band, who bounced accolades off of him, and for Sam that was a great feeling. He and Arleen visited great restaurants and the Follies Bergere. They went to the Eiffel Tower. Sam told Arleen, "Don't say I never take you anywhere."

DOWN UNDER IN AUSTRALIA

In Paris, Ed Leddy was back in the band. He wasn't playing lead, just relaxing with fifth trumpet parts. When he was fully recovered he resumed his first trumpet role. While in Paris, Ed and Sam went to the Besson factory, where great trumpets were made. They tried some horns. Ed had one that sounded great. Sam played it and he liked it too. Sam recalls, "Ed Leddy bought that horn for seventy-five dollars! Seventy-five dollars for a brand-new French Bresson! I asked the clerk if I could get the same horn. The clerk said he'd have it for me the next day."

A happy Sam and Ed left to catch a train to the shipping yard and the Queen Elizabeth. The next day Sam taxied to the factory. It was closed. It was May first, May Day, a big holiday there. Sam returned to the ship, really disappointed not to get that Besson.

Regardless, for Sam Noto the European gig ended with great satisfaction knowing the band was loved and that his friend Ed Leddy would bring a Besson trumpet to the States. Sam says, "I fondly remember Ed Leddy as a religious man who attended a Catholic college and who later had a spiritual storefront in San Francisco. But I've lost track of him. I don't know if he's alive. I don't think so, but I know he's quit playing."

Unlike what the Notos experienced when the Queen Elizabeth sailed from New York, the return trip was beautiful and with calm weather, they were on deck much of the time. The band checked in to the President Hotel in New York. Arleen would spend a few days there before leaving, and Sam would remain on the road. On a warm day Sam and Arleen walked, seeking a place to dine. From various storefronts they heard weird sounds; the genesis of 'rock' was upon them. Elvis Presley was now America's king of music, and music as Sam Noto knew it had changed. Jazz had lost its appeal. What Sam and Arleen heard was depressing, but Sam had to deal with it.

In New York, Kenton addressed the band and told them that before they left they would record an album. Sam, who vividly remembers that session says, "We were recording form eight in the morning till two in the afternoon; six hours a day for six days, and then a seventh day for another six hours. That's when we did the Cuban Fire album. Johnny Richards, the arranger, was writing all this stuff for Stan while we were in Europe so we rehearsed and recorded bit by bit. There was one chart on that album called 'El Congo Caliente.' The band knew it and played it in England and Europe. Every other tune was a new one. There was much sight-reading at rehearsals. That session was different; the music was hard. Those two days were tough. If you've heard Cuban Fire, you know it wasn't easy music, but we got through it. Vinnie Tano, Carl Fontana, Bill Perkins, Lennie Niehaus, and I soloed. That was the only playing we did in New York. There weren't any club gigs with the exception of one night somewhere in New Jersey."

From there, the band was on the road for several months of one-nighters. Ed Leddy was now splitting the lead with Sam, who thought Ed was losing interest. Sam says, "I told Ed, 'do what you want, you can take it all,' but he insisted we split it."

After the tortuous gigs the band returned to California to disband again. That was in late 1956. Everyone, including Stan Kenton, was tired. Sam Noto returned to grind out a living at the Palace. Joe Pizzuto was on piano, Dave Anacone was drummer, and sax man Bill Wullin was now the leader. When Sam took time off Pizzuto, who doubled on trumpet, replaced him, and Stan Opel replaced Pizzuto on piano. Sam says, "Dave Anacone on drums was good. The girls loved him. He caught all the bumps and grinds."

Sam was grateful for the Palace gig, rough as it was. He was supporting his young family. In February 1957, Stan Kenton called. "Sam, the band is going to Australia to do thirteen gigs in one month, and you will earn $1,000.00 a week playing lead. It will be you, Kent Larsen, Lenny Niehaus, Chuck Flores, and Bill Perkins. I'm augmenting the band with Australian players. Are you interested?" Sam quickly agreed.

Kenton said, "Great! I'll send you a plane ticket. Meet us April first at noon in Los Angeles at the Capitol Records building."

Sam wistfully told me, "Here I go again. I flew to Los Angeles and checked into a hotel near the big round Capitol Records building, which at the time was pretty much the face of Hollywood. At the meeting Kenton told us that this was a package tour. This meant the band would open the show, play for thirty minutes, and be finished. That was a dream gig! Thirty minutes and one concert a night playing music we already knew but had to practice to keep our chops up. We'd have time off. It would be great! The next morning we flew to Hawaii on a 1957 propeller driven plane. It was a fantastic trip. Then it was on to the Fiji Islands to re-fuel. The trip took thirty-six hours—in a prop! We were on the other side of the world. They had a buffet for us, and native women presented us with leis. That was something! From there we went to Sydney, Australia. We checked in and had two nights off before rehearsing with the Australian musicians.

"It was April, and in Australia that's autumn. It was warm. I'm on the beach, checking out the scenery. A bell rings; people are running out of the water. I didn't know why. I asked a local, and he said, 'Oh it's nothing, just a shark alert.' Oh man, there's a shark roaming around, a bell rings, everyone splits from the water! That was something. The food there was much better than the food in England. Australia had fantastic, beautiful, inexpensive steaks. The most expensive food was chicken. There's an abundance of cattle there, and I guess not too many chicken farms."

A rehearsal was scheduled for the next morning. Upon waking, Sam took up his trumpet case. It felt funny. It was heavier than normal. In a mirror he saw his left eye swollen completely shut. He touched it; it looked like he had been beaten. Sam says, "It looked like my eye was sticking out of my face. It was closed and puffed up, way out. Kenton saw me and was shocked. He said, 'Sam, what happened? Were you in a fight?' I said no, that I had woken up like this."

Kenton took Sam to a pharmacist who looked at Sam's eye and asked him if he'd eaten any shellfish. Sam had not, and at that point Kenton cancelled the rehearsal.

The next day Sam's swelling diminished, but his eyelids had two red bites. He soon learned that they weren't bites. In Australia, mosquitos are as big as bumble bees and Sam was allergic to them.

With the swelling gone the band began rehearsing. Sam recalls, "It turned out to be a fun gig; good paying, not a lot of work, and great food. When it ended I went home with almost $4,000.00. I bought a few things and an opal ring for Arleen."

KENTON AND BACK TO BALBOA

In 1957, after a Palace stint, Sam and Arleen brought their son Michael and Andrew, their newest son, born in 1954, to Balboa Beach, California, where Sam would join Kenton at the Rendezvous Ballroom. That gig was to mark Kenton's triumphant return to a venue that had brought him seminal fame sixteen years earlier. Anticipating large crowds, Kenton leased the ballroom for a year. The band would play six nights a week, record occasionally, tour nearby, and hang their hats at the Rendezvous, and for them, that was pleasurable.

Sam says, "I loved Balboa Beach, a beautiful place near the Pacific Ocean. While preparing for the gig I rented a furnished apartment for my family, after which I soloed on a Kenton album for Capitol Records entitled Back to Balboa."

The following are liner notes for the original LP release:
"It was late in 1957 that the Rendezvous became home base for the Kenton Orchestra. Balboa offered the stimulating surroundings; the Rendezvous offered a location spot between tours and incomparable acoustical properties. The body of sound and the crystal clear overtones achieved in this album are attributed to the orchestra's blowing over a block-long, polished dance floor and reverberating from the great arched wooden ceiling. The effect, without the use of echo chambers or electronic magic is one which seemingly places the listener within the walls of the pastel hall."

In a July 10, 1958 review, Down Beat Magazine critic Don Gold wrote, "Kenton, in describing Holman's 'Royal Blue' in the notes, terms it exciting, powerful, and positive. He could have been describing this band. In Perkins, Kamuca, Niehaus, Noto, and Katzman Kenton has several key soloists. Most of the charts in this LP are by Johnny Richards at his best. Other charts, by Marty Paich and Holman, take advantage of the orchestra's capabilities too. The vivid over-all Kenton sound is precisely executed. This is an important orchestra."

Unfortunately, though the reviews were positive, Kenton's Return to Balboa gig was a huge failure. Attendance was next to nothing. Kenton's dream of a repeat Rendezvous conquest was shattered. Sam says, "Nobody came. We played one night a week; Saturday. Stan pulled the plug, chalked it up to a bad investment, and the band broke up again."

When asked how the band responded, Sam said sadly, "Speaking personally? How can you maintain trumpet chops, velocity, playing one night a week? We had to practice all day just to emulate and maintain the strength needed to play six nights but getting paid for one. When it ended I was starving financially to the point of desperation. Fortunately, I was paid for the Balboa album and did a couple of record dates in LA, and for me that was it."

Prior to the Rendezvous demise, Arleen Noto received a telephone call. Her younger brother, Merton Christian, a member of the U.S. Navy, while on furlough in Buffalo, was killed in an automobile accident. Sam, remembering the late Merton who was only twenty years old says, "He was a great kid, home on leave, has an accident and dies; very sad."

It was Christmas time when Arleen and the boys returned to Buffalo for the funeral. Sam, alone and distraught by the turn of events and by Merton's death, knew that Christmas would be unhappy. On Christmas Day, while watching TV in his apartment, Sam heard a knock on his door. Kenton's trumpet section was there doing Christmas carols. "C'mon, you're with us," they said. "You won't be alone on this day." They all went and played carols in front of Stan Kenton's home in Beverly Hills. That saved Sam, who by his own admission was suffering a bout of self-pity. Soon Arleen, having left the boys with her parents, returned. With sixteen hundred dollars that Arleen had saved they bought a brand-new Volkswagen and drove it to Buffalo. After spending thirty-two dollars on gasoline, they were home.

IT WAS 1958

The year began, and until Sam, Arleen, and the boys found a place of their own, they stayed with Arleen's parents in nearby Attica, New York. Sam learned that some friends, tenor man Larry Covelli, Dick Mecca, Louie Marino, Tom Azarello, and a local tenor man Sam didn't know whose name was Don Menza, had the "New Jazz Quintet" at Bafo's. Sam told Arleen he wanted to see them and let everyone know he was around. Sam recalls, "I walked into Bafo's and they're playing, and playing good. When they got off the stand and saw me, oh man it was a celebration. I was introduced to Menza who said he was soon returning to Germany to live and did I want to take his place?"

Sam replaced Menza, and ultimately Wade Legge replaced Mecca on the piano. Sam says, "Mecca was a great jazz piano man, but Wade was a nationally known jazz piano giant formerly with Miles Davis and Dizzy Gillespie." The group, now under Sam's leadership, was making some great sounds. They had four nights at Bafo's, one at the Royal Arms, and one at Latona's. Sam says, "We were really getting into the jazz thing. We went to a friend's house, Jack Smith's, to tape record a chart of mine, and some of Wade's, and with Jack's equipment the tapes turned out fine."

While this was happening, Stan Kenton called Sam and asked if he'd return for a tour, but by now Sam was really down on big bands. Sam says, "I told Stan I wasn't coming back. Stan, I've got the city's hottest group and we're playing jazz—jazz, jazz, and more jazz—and everyone loves it."

Sam Noto knew the Stan Kenton gig was never stable. The band went out for several months and then hibernated for several months. Kenton frequently broke up the band. He drank a lot and needed to rest. Kenton knew Sam was excited about his small group, and he reluctantly accepted Sam's answer, knowing the local jazz gigs made Sam happy.

Sam says, "One night at the Royal Arms, I'm digging Wade's solo, and a bus pulls up in front. It's the Stan Kenton Orchestra bus. The band finished a gig in Canada and they've come to hear us. Stan Kenton enters, waves to me, and he listens. I leave the stand to greet him, and he says, 'Sam, how have you been? You sound great as ever, and this band, it's marvelous. What a great group! Now I know why you won't come back, and that piano man is fantastic. Do you have a tape of this band?'"

Sam told him that he did. "Stan wrote something on a piece of paper, handed it to me and said, 'I want you to go to New York City to see Teddy Reig there at this number and this building. Get in touch with him. He's a good friend who's producing a lot of Miles Davis records.'"

Sam Noto drove to New York City to see Teddy Reig. Don Menza, who had returned from Germany, was in town and went with him. Upon arriving, Menza asked Sam if he could take the car to Long Island to see Rose.

"Whoa, Long Island?" Sam asked.

"Yeah, that's where she lives. I'll do that while you do your business."

Menza and the beautiful Rose Yarusso, whom Menza subsequently married, were classmates at Fredonia State College. Sam says, "He took my Volks while I have this meeting with Teddy Reig at his office. We talk, and Reig puts the tape on. But as he does he picks up the phone and talks to someone. I'm thinking, 'C'mon, are you going to listen to this thing or not? I mean, c'mon!'

"Teddy Reig says, 'The band sounds pretty good, but we're not selling any white jazz right now.' I say, 'What?' He says, 'Stan Kenton's a good friend of mine, but I must tell you, business is business. The band's good but there's nobody in it.' I said, 'That piano man is Wade Legge. He played with Dizzy Gillespie, with Miles, Sonny Rollins, and was the original piano with Clifford Brown and Sonny, but he was a strange dude. He quit because he wanted equal billing.' Teddy Reig responded, 'As I said, the group sounds real good, but we're not selling any white jazz, we're selling the big guys, the black artists.' "

Sam was shot down and shot down quick. Teddy Reig didn't recognize the great white players. They were in the back seat because it was black music all the time. In another era, Beiderbecke was a great white trumpet player, but everyone adored Louis Armstrong. When Don Menza returned for Sam he saw that Sam was down, depressed. Sam told him what happened. Menza said, "Man, what did you expect?"

He tried cheering Sam up, and asked if he could drive.

Sam said, "Drive, man, drive."

While on the highway, Menza stopped the car and said, "Sam, watch this." With his hand he struck a cardboard box in the back seat, and sounds were heard. Sam said, "What's in there?"

Menza said, "Clams, I got 'em on the beach and they're on ice."

Back in Buffalo Sam kept his group intact but problems occurred. Wade Legge was arrogant. He wasn't interested in what the others were doing. He approached Sam one night after a set and said, "Sam, come here, you know, man since I joined the group you sound a lot better."

Sam said, "Yeah, Wade, sure yeah, you're right."

Ultimately the group's popularity waned, and without public interest it crumbled like some things did for Sam Noto.

TRUCK DRIVING AND WOODY HERMAN

1959 arrived, and with it came a day job for Sam. He was driving a dump truck courtesy of his father-in-law, Arthur Christian, who had arranged a try-out and a Teamsters Union membership. Arthur said, "Don't do anything, just drive. They tell you to pick up anything you don't pick up anything! You don't do nothing but drive!"

Stan Kenton's star trumpet artist, whose creative jazz brilliance thrilled British and European royalty, would now drive a dump truck. He did so for a few horrendous weeks. Dumping loads of various materials in dirt and mud filled areas, things of that nature, and often in the rain, it was rough, but it was a job. It was a job in which he earned more than he ever did playing. Sam says, "Driving a stick shift with a big load was kind of, well…let me say it wasn't easy, that's for sure. I told my father-in-law, 'I don't want to do this. I can't hack it. I'm quitting.' "

He then relayed his decision to Arleen. She said, "Sam, it's up to you." As she did, the phone rang. It was Joe Romano, a dear old friend and marvelous tenor man from Rochester. (In a few years he would come to Bafo's with Chuck Mangione to play with Sam.) At the moment Joe was in Woody Herman's band. Romano asked Sam what he was doing. Sam told Joe he was driving a dump truck but thinking of quitting.

"Sam, give me a break."

Sam said, "That's what I'm doing."

Romano said, "Sam, I'm in Woody's band, do you want to join us?"

Sam responded, "I'll join anybody's band."

Joe said, "Don Lanphere's on tenor too, remember him? He was with Fats Navarro. You dug Fats like you dug Dizzy. But man, I'll tell you, Woody's not a jazz band anymore. We do dances, Woody had tax problems. A road manager stole all his bread and never paid the IRS. Willie Thomas is the new road manager. He's here; I'll let you talk to him."

Joe put Willie on the phone and Willie said, "Yeah, Sam, I heard all about you, man. Come on the band and play first trumpet." Sam said he would and asked what the chair paid.

"One hundred and sixty-five bucks," said Willie. "And I'm giving you a ten buck raise right now, before you even come. You'll get one hundred seventy-five. Meet us down in Miami."

Sam flew to Miami to replace the amazing Bill Chase. Arriving at Willie's hotel Sam rang his room. Willie answered and said, "Yeah, come on up. I'm in Room 2711."

Sam says, "The door opened, and Willie Thomas stuck a pipe with a deep load of stuff in my mouth and said, 'You're going to love this band.'" Sam went on, "Later in life Willie was reduced to selling cocaine on the floor of the Musician's Union in New York City, and I think he was busted."

Upon joining Woody, Sam would truly learn the meaning of Romano's words. The band was a dance band playing dance music. A reflective Sam says, "Woody was bad news all the time; terrible shape, unhappy, and always down. He lost his home to the IRS, they took everything. I think Sinatra bailed him out. I wasn't having any fun. And Joe was apologizing, 'I'm sorry, Sam.' " Sam says, "Jokingly, I told him not to call me anymore."

Sam often thinks of those days with Woody. It was a dance band, but it was a good one, even without jazz. They'd slip in one or two to blow on. One night, Sam soloed on a ballad, but didn't play the melody; he did as he did with Clyde McCoy, what he did best—he played a jazz solo. He saw Woody staring at him. He sat down. Woody leaned over the trombone section, eyes locked on Sam. Sam leaned forward, almost face to face with Woody, who said, "Hardly danceable."

"What?" said Sam.

"Hardly danceable," Woody repeated.

Sam says, "That year, Romano and I were in some town in Iowa on Woody's band leaving a gig and going to Des Moines. It's pitch dark, the middle of the night, and we're traveling. What else can you do on a bus? Read? Reading on a moving bus gave me a headache. Then again, you can also drink yourself to sleep. Joe and me were in the back of the bus playing poker, and hitting the vodka pretty good. But we were getting sleepy. Joe said, 'I've gotta pee.' There was no john on the bus. So, Joe goes to the bus driver and asks if we could make a pee stop. The driver wouldn't stop. He was concerned about getting to Des Moines and felt he was behind schedule. Joe insisted that he had to pee. The driver asked if Joe could pee in a cup and throw it out the window. Joe said, 'No! Stop the bus!' The driver, now angry, stopped the bus and lurched it a bit. Joe, who was wacked out, fell into a seat. We leave the bus, pee, and the bus drives off.

"A few hours later the bus is quiet. Everyone's sleeping, the sun is rising. Joe Romano is moaning, complaining about a pain in his gut. Jack Sixt, the bass player, a big guy, thinks Joe has to throw up from drinking too much. He has Joe by the belt and pushes him up and down, trying to get him to puke. Joe is in extreme pain. I told Jack, 'Don't do that, something is wrong with Joe.' "

It was Saturday morning, and a big Notre Dame football game was to be played in Des Moines later that day. There were no motel rooms, and the band stayed at an Army barracks. Joe Romano was still in severe pain. Sam says, "I told Woody and the upper echelon; they called an ambulance that took Joe to a hospital."

It was later learned that when the bus lurched and Joe fell into a seat, his bladder was full and it ruptured. Blood had mixed with his urine. His system had been poisoned, and without treatment he would have died. He was hospitalized, and Woody replaced him. Upon his release from the hospital, Joe returned to Rochester. Sam says, "I'd call to check on his progress and he'd say I saved his life because no one on that bus except me realized how sick he was. Whenever I saw Joe after that he'd say to anyone there, 'This guy saved my life,' and he'd tell the story."

Joe Romano and Sam Noto, the proverbial two peas in a jazz pod got along famously. Musically, that wasn't true of Sam and Woody Herman. They weren't friends. Sam told me, "One night Woody saw a beautiful woman alone on the dance floor. He told Joe Romano, 'You got it, Joe,' and left the stand. We're in the middle of a tune, and Woody makes Joe the leader and dances with this chick! When the tune finished I called for number 158, an up-tempo Al Cohn chart. I say, 'One, two, one, two, three, four,' and the band starts cooking. All the guys are dying, waiting for this. The band is burning and having fun. We finished, and the guys are jubilant. Woody comes on the stand and starts screaming at Joe, who said, 'Hey man, from now on lead your own x*#& band!'

"Joe Romano tended to be angry from time to time and would lose his temper, but Woody loved him. Later, Joe, me, and Louie Marinaccio did that whole Renaissance thing on Pearl Street in Buffalo, and I'll get to that later."

After a few months Woody's band broke up, and Sam left. Woody never said goodbye. Sam tells it this way, "That was it. I went one way and Woody the other. Back home I'm in the same notorious Noto bag; nothing, until a gig at the Chez Ami opened, and then that too fizzled. In 1960 Woody reorganized. Bill Chase came back and so did Sal Nistico, the great tenor man who turned on the whole band. Woody loved him. Sal would say, 'I'm like an eight-note machine here.' Woody gave Sal all the fast solos. That band was hot with him and Chase. Lots of guys came back, but I didn't."

Sam, remembering those days, takes us into the future to mention a Woody Herman experience from the 1980s when Sam lived in Toronto and played with Rob McConnell's Boss Brass. Sam says, "Oh man, I've got to tell you this, I almost forgot. Woody was in Toronto to do a gig, but without his band. He hired Boss Brass guys, which he would front, and I was among them. At a rehearsal Woody sees me in the trumpet section and waves. I was shocked! When I was on his band he wouldn't give me the time of day. At gig time when he opened up some charts for solos he always pointed to me to solo. In fact, some guys joked, 'What's this, the Sam Noto Show?' After the gig I went to a club where Zoot Sims was playing, and who's at the bar? Woody Herman. And I say, 'Hey Wood, how you doing?' He says, 'Sam, you played some great solos tonight.' I said, 'I didn't think you noticed.' He says, 'C'mon, have a drink.' I did, and we got drunk. He told me what he was going through while I was on his band. And I said, 'I know, Woody, I know all about it,' and we became good friends. Drunks, you either hate 'em or love 'em."

BACK TO THE GRIND

Between Kenton tours Sam found work, if not solace, at the Palace, and after Woody he was back. Drummer Dave Anacone was now the leader, but he was quitting to go into the saloon business. The Palace manager, Joe DiMartina, made Sam the leader at almost one hundred and eighty dollars a week. Sam told me, "Yeah, I was it. I had the great Bill Rasey on piano, Louie Marino on drums, and Larry Covelli on tenor. The band was really playing, and we loved it, except when the features—the chicks—come on. Some of them would say, do you know this tune or that tune, so we'd play, and we'd blow. At one rehearsal a chick, a low-level stripper, one the comics used as a foil said, 'I haven't any music, but can you do a chorus of this and two choruses of that, and then close with that one?' I told her we could do that. So, we're first in the morning show. We're playing, and that chick comes out. I look up and she can't even walk, let alone dance. She was the worst. The audience, consisting of two derelicts, didn't even applaud. We leave the pit while the comics are on, and we go downstairs. That no-talent chick comes in screaming 'You sons of bitches!' I said, 'Wait a minute, what's the matter?' She said, 'You played my music wrong! I didn't get any applause!' I said, 'Oh, you thought it was the music?' I told her it was because she couldn't dance. She screamed, 'You destroyed me!' and she left. I followed her. My balls are broken. When the guys see I'm in her face they said, 'Sam, cool it.' I blew up. I was ready to go. I hit the plasterboard door of her little cubbyhole and it broke. She saw that, backed off and ran to management. I said to the guys, 'Well, there goes the gig.'

"So, as we're leaving to play horseshoes at Rinaldo's, here comes Joe DiMartina who says, 'Sam, is everything worked out?' I said, 'Joe, I'll tell you why I hit the door.' He said, 'You hit the door? Did you hurt your hand?' I said I didn't. That was the end of it. Joe liked me. I remember once he said, 'Canadians pack the place, and when they leave they never mention the girls, only how much they love the band.' Everyone loved the band."

Sam Noto remembered his prior Palace days, when he played with Roy Ricotta, Sam Sokoloff, and Bill Wullin. But now the world traveler was the newly appointed king of a different Palace, where through the years Blaze Starr, Tempest Storm, and Sally and Her Snakes performed to "A Pretty Girl is Like a Melody." That song was sung there a few decades before by Joseph Levich, aka Jerry Lewis, and by Alphonso Giuseppe Giovanni Roberto D'Abruzzo, aka Robert Alda, before they became famous. Sam told me his favorite Palace anecdote concerns the time when trombonist Ang Callea, a one-week addition to the band, was in the pit near the apron of the stage doing his thing for Sally and Her Snakes. Sam says, "We were wailing on 'An American in Paris.' Suddenly I see one of Sally's snakes approaching the lit area of the apron. 'Ang! Watch it!' I yell. Ang looks up, sees the snake and screams, 'baaayaaaa!' He ran from the pit, horn and all."

Sam continues, "After the European tour, late '56 or early '57, and before the Australian gig, I'm at the Palace. I go home for dinner, and I get a call from a guy in Rochester who owns a jazz club there. He asked what I was doing. I told him I was working at the Palace Theater. He wanted to know if I could come to his place that night. 'Rochester?' I asked, 'tonight? Why?' He said, 'Freddie Hubbard, the trumpet player is here with his group, and he's got an attitude about how great he is. He's pissing me off. He won't play unless he feels like it, and when he does, and finishes, he takes long breaks.' I asked him what he expected me to do. He said, 'I want you to come here and play with him.' I said, 'You want me to play with Freddie Hubbard?! Are you crazy? I have to go back to work. I'm on my dinner break.' The owner said, 'Whatever bread you make at The Palace I'll take care of it. Just come and sit in with him.' I asked him, 'How do you know Freddie Hubbard will let me sit in? He's Freddie Hubbard, he doesn't know me or who the hell I am.' He said, 'Sam, if you do me this favor you could bring friends and all drinks are on me. I'll pay you and cover whatever you pay your Palace sub. I just want this son-of-a-bitch to know that there's a guy around here as good, if not better than him!' "

Thinking it would be different as opposed to the pit, Sam agreed. The next day, he, Larry Covelli, Frankie Bifulco, Joe Marfoglio, and Louie Marinaccio drove to Rochester. Freddie Hubbard was finishing a set when Sam and his friends entered the club. Sam says, "I brought my horn into the kitchen, and the guys and I went to the bar. As we do, Freddie Hubbard, who saw us enter, and saw me with my case, said over the mike, 'Well, we're going to take a short break right now, but from what I understand there's a local yokel who's going to sit in with me, some dodo, or dough dough; something like that.' "

Sam says, "He starts with that bullshit. The guys, puzzled, look at me. I say to myself, 'what the fuck is it with this guy?' The club owner brings Freddie over and introduces him to me, and he has a real attitude. He said, 'I hear you play trumpet, man. You want to come play a couple tunes with me, man? Sure, okay, you can.' I waited till he goes on. I'm angry that over the mike he was disrespectful to me, busting my balls like that. He's a great player, but you're not supposed to be that kind of a guy. I went into the kitchen for my horn and got on the bandstand. Freddie Hubbard said, 'We're gonna play Blues in A Flat,' and he starts playing. He blew, then the sax, and then me. I played like I always do, but by then I was angrier and played with a vengeance, and I got applause. Freddie comes to me and said, 'What kind of mouthpiece is that, man?' I said, 'It's a mouthpiece, what do you want from me?' Now over the mike Freddie said, 'Let's give a big hand for Sam Noto.' He pronounced my name correctly. Then he told the saxophone player, 'Take a break, Sam Noto and I are going to play.' We played three full tunes and tore the house apart. That made the Buffalo guys really proud." Sam smiled. "After that Freddie had an entirely different attitude. He was even friendly."

THE APPLE, MENZA, AND BIG MOTHERS

In 1960, Kenton called Sam Noto and asked him to tour in a concert series: Stan Kenton versus Count Basie. Sam, who a few years before had told Kenton he'd had it with big bands, accepted the gig, "Stan had some good guys," he said. "Bud Brisbois, Dalton Smith on trumpet, and tenor man Sam Donahue. I was on the band for a few months. It featured Brisbois and Donahue having a high note trumpet/sax battle; that was the band's so-called jazz. I was cynical. Listening to Count Basie every night was fun. Stan tried playing more jazz because Basie's music was hot and burning up the theaters, but it wasn't enough, and I quit the band."

In his heart, an emotional Sam Noto knew this was his musical farewell to Kenton, a man to whom he felt he owed so much. Sam felt like Mickey Rooney, leaving Boy's Town forever. Nonetheless, he came home to a bad gig situation.

Sam says, "I talked to Arleen. I told her that work in Buffalo was vanishing. I said, 'There's nothing here, even the Town Casino is cutting down. How about we move to New York City; I can find work around there.' Arleen said, 'Don't you have to join the musician's union there too to do that?' I said, 'Yeah, you're right. I'll do that. I'll call Tony Ragusa who lives there. I'll tell him what's happening, what's going down, what I intend to do, and ask if I can use his New York address. If he says okay, I'll put my card into Local 802, and that'll be it.'"

Sam spoke to Tony Ragusa who said, "Yeah Sam, don't worry about it, do it." Sam says, "With Tony's help, it's like I'm living in

New York City. You can't leave once your card is in, but I did. Tony said the union called once and asked for me, but he told them I wasn't home. They never called again. After the required three-month wait, in the summer of 1960, Sam Noto was a member of New York City's Musician's Local 802. Luckily, while in Buffalo he was hired to play at Melody Fair, a successful summer tent north of the city. It was a good gig. The band played for Nat Cole, Maynard Ferguson's band, and Don Rickles. One night after a show, Sam drove to Big Mother's, a bar on Main Street near the University of Buffalo, where Don Menza had a trio, him, bass, and drums.

Sam told me, "Menza saw me and said, 'Hey man, you got your horn?' I did. The place was crowded, lots of UB kids, and the place had real good food, sandwiches, stuff like that, and lots of beer and wine. I sat in. We played a couple of tunes, and the guy who owned the place heard me. He came over and asked Don who I was. Don said, 'Gus, this is Sam Noto. He's played with Stan Kenton and Woody Herman.' Gus offered me a job there and I took it. So, we started playing as a quartet. The place was busy, all those school kids coming in. We went up to three nights a week, then four nights. Larry Covelli sat in, and Gus says, 'Who's this?' Menza said, 'This is Larry Covelli, he's sitting in.' Gus says, 'Hire him, too—but no more sitting in.'

"We were now a quintet, and around that time we recorded a tune called Spanish Boots that was on many local jukeboxes. Don was always taping what we played. He still has those tapes, and now, when we meet, he talks about them, 'Sam, we sounded pretty good back then.' We ended up playing six nights a week at Big Mother's for many months, playing more and more jazz. That's when I really started getting into it, with no piano. I learned to cross the bass line, and began taking liberties, and started creating my own kind of jazz."

"Big Mother's was a dream gig," says Sam. "But after a few months, maybe five or six, what's his name, Gus, he split, and we got stiffed for the last week we played, and the place went down. I don't know what happened. By then, Ang Callea and Paul Faulise, a trombonist who lived in New York City, were in the pit of the Broadway musical, Music Man. Ang was staying with Paul. So, when I got the 802 card Paul told Frank Vaccaro, another Buffalo trombonist who was in the band in a famous New York City nightclub called The Latin Quarter. Frank Vaccaro called and asked if I wanted the gig at The Latin Quarter. I said, 'Yeah man, yeah.'

"I went to New York, and later I'd send for Arleen and our two sons. I found an apartment in Brooklyn. I put a down payment on it. At the time, The Latin Quarter bandleader was Joe Lombardi, a strict old guy. We played behind a scrim, but when the curtain opened the band was visible to the audience. Joe Lombardi said, 'When the audience sees you I don't want anybody drinking water, nothing.' That was a hard gig. We played for a line of girls. My mouth was dry. I had a bottle of water under my chair. I took a drink, and Joe saw me. 'You're fired! You're fired!' After the gig he called me into his room. I said, 'Joe, I'm a human being, I ran out of saliva, I couldn't play. What's the difference? I drank some water to help me.' "

Lombardi retracted the notice, and Sam remained on the job. He stayed with Angelo and Paul in Paul's apartment. When he'd leave for the Latin Quarter gig, which was six hours long, Ang and Paul's Music Man gig would have just ended. They were in pajamas, drinking martinis, and eating. When he'd return, they were still in pajamas, drinking and eating.

While Sam was at The Latin Quarter, a Canadian who wanted to record him said, "Be at this studio at such and such a time." Sam went there, and nothing was happening. He called the Canadian who said, "We decided to go with Grant Green, the black guitarist." All Sam thought of was his meeting with Teddy Reig, and as he did, a phone call came from his mother-in-law. She said, "Arleen was rushed to the hospital. She had a pregnancy caught in her fallopian tube; it erupted and she's bleeding internally." Sam told Joe Lombardi, "I've got to go back, my wife is ill." Lombardi said, "Yes, okay, go, and if you want to come back you can. I'll get someone to sub for you." Upon leaving The Latin Quarter, the band presented Sam with two hundred and twenty dollars in an envelope that read, "Hurry back, hope everything's okay."

Back home, Arleen's situation was remedied, but she was depressed, and wouldn't move to New York City. Sam didn't return to The Latin Quarter. The union card plan proved to be a waste of time and money.

COUNT BASIE

Nothing of any import worked out for Sam Noto between 1960 and 1964. They were tough years, hollow, and filled with near endless bouts of depression. He was dealing with where he was as a musician, and the knowledge that Arleen wouldn't leave for New York or Los Angeles. It was dilemma time; Sam was between the proverbial rock and the hard place he knew so well. He worked one summer at the Glen Casino with Moe Balsom's abbreviated Town Casino band. Sam reflects, "We played for some good acts; comedians, singers, people like that." In addition to that Sam did what he could to make ends meet. But more importantly, he knew he had to make a move, and knew it had to be drastic— like leaving town. It was that or a day job, and for the moment, an unemployed world-class jazz musician in Buffalo, New York, was planning and thinking of a way to support his family.

In 1961 when Music Man ended on Broadway, Ang Callea was back home. He and Sam were hanging at Dugan's, a bar on Elmwood Avenue. They had a few jam sessions there. Sam was still trying to play his music on a larger scale. He questioned the path he was on, what was he doing? He was consumed with thoughts; where am I? Who am I? They lingered in his mind, such as it was. He was in his thirties, and he knew he must find a remedy and figure something out.

In 1964, at the height of Sam's problems, came a phone call. Don Rader, a trumpet player in Count Basie's orchestra, couldn't cross the border into Canada from Buffalo for a gig in Toronto.

Rader couldn't enter Canada because he had been arrested years ago for possession of marijuana while in Maynard Ferguson's band in Montreal. The caller asked Sam to sub for Rader that night on Basie's Toronto gig. He would be paid one hundred and fifty dollars. Sam accepted and was told to meet Mr. Snodgrass, the band manager, at the ballroom where they were to perform. Knowing that his car couldn't make the ninety mile trip, Sam asked Ang Callea to drive him.

At the ballroom, Mr. Snodgrass told Sam he was to sit in Rader's chair, the "Thad Jones" chair. Sam says, "I got up there and Basie started playing, and just by his intro the band knew the tune. Me? I was totally befuddled. I didn't know what was happening. I looked at the guy next to me; 'what's up? What's up?' The band's playing, and I'm going crazy looking for charts on my stand. Those guys played those charts so often they didn't need stands, they were only there for the show. Finally, when I found my chart and my place, I contributed to the session and spit out a solo on a Basie classic—'Jumping at the Woodside.' It was a short one at the bridge, the middle of the tune. I know I turned a few heads. Ang was in the audience digging it. When the band took a break, Ang and I did our number, drinking beer or whatever we could get our hands on."

When the gig ended, Mr. Snodgrass paid Sam and thanked him graciously. Sam told me, "That was it. A day or two later my phone rang. I picked it up and said hello."

A voice said, "Sim?"

"Who?"

Again, the voice said, "Sim?"

"Yeah, this is Sam."

"This is Base."

"Who? Who is this? What? Who is it?"

The voice said, "This is Base."

"Who?"

The voice said, "Count Basie, man, Count Basie!"

Sam recalls that he laughed aloud. Basie cracked him up. He said, "Oh yeah, Base, how you doing man?" Base asked him where he had gone the other night, Sam told him, "I got paid and went back to Buffalo."

"You couldn't come and talk to old Base?"

Sam replied, "Oh Base, I'm sorry man, my friend drove me, and he wanted to split."

Basie said, "Well, I'd like to have you on the band."

Sam was quick to say that Don Rader was a friend, and that he wouldn't take the job from him. Basie told him that Don was leaving and that he wanted Sam to take his place. So, Sam agreed to do it. Basie promised to be in touch and to let him know what was happening.

Soon after, Basie called and told him to buy a plane ticket to Pittsburgh. He would pay Sam back when he got there, and Sam was to meet the band at The William Penn Hotel. Sam flew to Pittsburgh, grabbed a taxi to Basie's hotel, and went to his room. Basie reimbursed him and said, "I love how you play, and I'm glad you're on the band."

The first few months with Count Basie were marvelous. Playing jazz in the band was pure joy. They played their music in black clubs and an occasional dance hall all over the South. Musically they were burning, ripping the South apart. The more they played, the better they were, and for Sam Noto it was a great time. But it was one that would soon end.

The cold, harsh, unsentimental winds of change were dancing in the air. Basie was aging. He no longer wanted the worries and the responsibilities of leadership. His musicians learned that the band had been sold to the Willard Alexander Theatrical Agency, and Basie was merely a front with a good salary. The agency booked the band, and Basie did what he was told. Suddenly these fine jazz players were backing up singers; four weeks with Keely Smith at the Coconut Grove in LA, and then Tony Bennett. Those great musicians in what was once Count Basie's jazz band were now ordinary players, obscured in a not so extraordinary backup band.

In 1964 they played a tune or two to open various shows. Basie had it made. He left the stand. Singers usually had their own pianist conductors, and what remained of the show was the singer. Sam Noto was disillusioned.

"They say I have a reputation for disliking singers," Sam ponders. "Maybe it's because I've always thought they ruined the Big Band Era. It was an industry, and they destroyed it; it took over the whole thing. I'm talking about Sinatra, Jo Stafford, all of them, the really good singers. People just went to see them and didn't care about the great Big Bands. Basie stopped doing his thing; no jazz, just singers all the time. I didn't want to do that. I was there to play with Count Basie, a jazz musician. Trombonist Billy Byers was on the band. He was a great arranger and he wrote beautiful charts.

"I knew we were going to Las Vegas to do two weeks at the Sands. I thought we were to play jazz. On the bus to Vegas Basie came by and said, 'Sam, you're going to play with your boy now.' I said, 'My boy? Basie, don't call me boy.' Basie laughed and sat next to me. He liked me, and I liked him. He was a beautiful cat. Basie said, 'No, no man, I'm sorry. I should've said 'your boy Frank'. Frank Sinatra, man.' I said, 'Base, why do you think Sinatra's my boy? Who told you that?' Basie laughed and said, 'I don't know, Sam, but we're playing for him at the Sands.'

"Opening night we're there. I think it was an invitation only type event. The band is to play a couple of tunes before Sinatra comes out. That was the Basie gig: backing Sinatra. Eddie 'Lockjaw' Davis, the road manager and great tenor man, comes in before we're to play and said, 'Sam, our opening tune will be Shiny Stockings.' I said, 'That's my solo.' Jaws said that he knew, and that Basie wanted me to play it in front of the band. I was amazed. Only a few saxophones do that because the mikes are there. Trumpets and trombones all soloed from their section. I said, 'Jaws, are you sure Basie wants me to play in front?' He said, 'Yeah man, he wanted me to tell you, play the solo in front.' "

It's Sinatra's opening night, and Sam plays his "Shiny Stockings" solo in front, up close and personal to a huge appreciative audience of movie stars and famous people. Basie looked appreciatively at Sam. Sam says, "I looked at Basie, and if he looks at you after a solo, you know he liked what you played. If he didn't, he didn't like it. After the show I'm in the casino and I'm hitting the slots. Jaws sees me, and he said, 'Sam, from now on you've got to play the solo from the back, from the section.' I said, 'Why? Did Basie change his mind?' Jaws said, 'No man, Sinatra said something to Basie about it. Frank told him to tell you he's the star. It's one of those things.' "

Sam didn't know what or why that was because Sinatra wasn't even on stage yet. It was Basie's band playing, but for now Sam soloing in front was over. The two weeks with Sinatra went well. When the gig ended, Sinatra threw a party for the band and many others. Sam Noto, who vividly remembers that night, says, "The place was swinging. People were having a great time. I was at the bar with Billy Byers, and I was drinking a lot. In the mirror behind the bar, I see Basie and Sinatra coming toward us. Basie said, 'Sam?' Sam says, 'I didn't turn around, and this time Basie says, 'Sam, I want you to meet someone.' ' I didn't turn around. I was bugged. My third son, Andrew, was four years old. I hadn't seen him in so long, and I was annoyed playing for singers."

Frank Sinatra said to Sam, "Hey corn cob." Sam says, "I didn't laugh. I didn't do anything. I just died of embarrassment, and I knew Basie knew." Sinatra said to Basie, "What's with this guy? What's with him, huh? What's with him?" Sam says, "Basie must have known I was in a bad mood behind the solo thing, and he turned to Sinatra and said, 'He's not too happy,' and he hurried Sinatra away." Billy Byers said, "Sam, you got a set of balls." After that, Sam told Billy about the solo caper.

Sam says, "The next day Basie told the band they were doing another singer. I went to Basie and said, 'I'm going home.' Basie said, 'What do you mean?' I told him I was playing fewer and fewer solos. 'I won't play for singers anymore, and I want to see my youngest son. I'm giving my two weeks' notice.' Later, I told Jaws, who said, 'Sam, Basie doesn't like this.' I told him, 'I'm sorry. I'm not happy, that's it.'

"I'm in my room and I get a call from Basie. I go to his room and there's a pile of food and blow on the table. Basie says, 'Help yourself.' I took a little and then Basie said, 'So, you really want to leave?' I said I did. Basie said, 'I can appreciate you not liking singers, but I've got to keep the band working. You know how it is.' I said that I understood."

Sam Noto cherished Count Basie's friendship. Basie told him that if he ever wanted to come back to just call him. Sam thought he was just being courteous, and said, "Yeah, sure, Base, I'll do that." He finished his two weeks, and after five months he was finally back in Buffalo to see Arleen, his family, and his third son Andrew.

Sam says, "It was 1964, and I knew I had made another mistake when I saw what condition the city was in, jazz-wise.

Nothing was happening, and again I was despondent." Sam Noto fell into the Buffalo lag and thought he was going downhill for the last time. He recalls how he survived on the road with various bands. Musicians paid for their own food and lodging. Sam skimped to send most of what he earned to Arleen to take care of his family. At that time there was no per diem.

He talked to Arleen about his feelings. He told her, "Basie said if I wanted to come back all I have to do is call him." Arleen suggested he return to Basie. Sam, apprehensive, said, "I don't know, maybe he was just being nice. How do I know he meant it?" Arleen said, "Sam, you won't know till you call him."

Sam learned where Basie was appearing and called him. Basie was pleased to hear from him and said, "Sam, I'm not happy with what we have now. Let me work it out, and I'll get back to you." Soon after that conversation Basie called Sam, and he was back on Basie's band.

Sam reminisces about his first stint with Basie in New York when the marvelous tenor man Sal Nistico was on the band. Sam says, "Basie loved Sal, but he was strung out too often and was fired. That's when Basie hired Eddie 'Lockjaw' Davis to replace Sal and to be his road manager." The current Basie band had trumpeter Gene Gold splitting the lead with Sonny Cohen. Sam was back on the Thad Jones chair. They did some nice gigs and recorded an LP of pop tunes. The Willard Alexander Agency brought in tenor man Illinois Jaquet to play on the LP. Sam played a muted solo on some vague piece and thought the entire session was a waste of time. Sam says, "It was something any band of the day could have done. It wasn't the Basie jazz band. It had Basie's style and that was it."

After that they returned to the groove Sam despised. Sam says, "I was drinking pretty heavy and was bitching at the band guys about singers and the records they were playing on the band bus. We'd finish a gig, get on the bus, and they're playing Basie records. I told them, 'Hey, put some Charlie Parker on, we just played this stuff.' Some bandmates, knowing I was juiced, said, 'Sam, cool it man, cool it.'"

Soon after, Sam was a defendant in the Count Basie Kangaroo Court. Sam says, "We were in Des Moines, Iowa, at a combination party/press release thing with journalists and reporters. One, a young black woman, interviewed me about 'being white in a black man's orchestra.' I talked to her and saw the band guys looking over, snickering. After the event, when we got on the bus, I was served with papers. The band said I was being charged with fraternizing with a dog."

Sam Noto never understood the charge brought against him because, by his testimony, "the alleged dog looked pretty good to me." The jury, after deliberating, returned a guilty verdict. Sam was fined fifty dollars, but never paid it. He says, "A lot of guys on Basie's band disliked me, big time. I got along with Al Aarons, a beautiful guy and a real gentleman, and I liked guitarist Freddie Green. The more I soloed, the colder some of those guys got toward me. But Basie liked what I played. One night the bus stopped at a Howard Johnson's. Inside, Basie said to me, 'Sam, you don't look too happy.' I told him I was all right. Basie told me to sit down and he said, 'I'm going to tell you this one time, and one time only. Not everybody can love you, but Basie loves you.' I told him, 'Man, fuck these guys. They don't like me so fuck 'em.'"

Sam says, "Again, I was the only white guy on the band like the first time after Sal Nistico was fired. The prejudice was there. It was evident. You could feel it."

By his own admission, Sam was screwing up, and screwing up fairly well. A few times he was in Basie's face about things. Early in 1965 when the band arrived in New York City, Mr. Snodgrass told Sam, "Basie wants you to turn in your uniform." In the parlance of the big band trade that meant "you're going home." Sam was paid and flew to Buffalo, to maybe work at the Palace Burlesk.

Basie had been paying Sam three hundred and fifty dollars a week, and by mid-sixties standards that was exceptional. That was the most he had ever received per week with any band. Now that too had ended. Back home he was a lone passenger, freezing in a cold water vessel, one he was always in: devoid of income, dismal feelings, and no prospect for work.

THE PRINCE EDWARD ON PEARL STREET

Sam met with Frank St. George who once owned The Jazz Center, a musical loft on Washington Street. Frank was a lover of traditional jazz until he heard Sam's group at his place and converted to Sam's brand. He loved it, and he still loved his traditional players. Sam told him, "Frank, I'm home, and can't find any work after being in Count Basie's band." Frank told him that there was a place, the Prince Edward Hotel near the Greyhound bus terminal on Pearl Street. Frank said that he knew the owner and that he would talk to him about putting Sam in there with a small group.

Frank spoke to his friend, Tony Briandi, whose uncle Rocco Vaccaro owned the Prince Edward hotel. Sam says, "I went there. I knew Tony's brother, Angelo. We were teenagers together. We'd skip school to play pool on Grant Street. Angelo also played trumpet." After a brief conversation, Tony Briandi said, "If you want to give it a try, let's do a Friday and Saturday for a couple of weeks and see what happens." Sam asked Tony if he'd put an ad in the newspapers, and Tony said he would. Sam called the bass player, Tom Azarello, and told him that he'd gotten this gig and wanted to hire him. Sam asked, 'Who's in town?' Tom said he was playing around with his younger brother, Joe, and drummer Al Cecchi. Sam asked Tom if he could hire them for a Friday and Saturday gig at the Prince Edward Hotel, a gig that would start the next week. Tom Azarello agreed, and the following week the Sam Noto Quartet was appearing at the Prince Edward Hotel.

Sam says, "Believe it or not, people were showing up. Tony Briandi and his uncle were pretty happy. The money they paid my group wasn't much, but Tony promised that if it picked up, more would come." Sam says, "More people were coming in, and Tony told me he would keep his promise about a raise. I told him, 'Instead of a raise, give us the money; I'll add another player.' Tony agreed, and I hired Joe Romano on tenor as my fifth member, and he was allowed to occupy a room at the Prince Edward Hotel, which wasn't a hotel at all, but a glorified rooming house."

For Sam Noto, getting Romano there was a continuation of a long and beautiful friendship. The band's sound with his addition was even better. He and Sam wrote charts for the group, and with attendance getting even better, the gig would last for several months. Sam says, "We made a lot of friends there. Many West Side guys came in. Angelo Brandi was always there, as was Louie Marinaccio and Joe Insalacco. We had a following. They loved the band, and they loved Joe Romano's playing. I'll never forget, it was April 17, Sunday, 1965—my birthday. We were playing a two o'clock jam session. The day before, I bought a magnum of champagne to celebrate with the guys on Sunday afternoon. I parked my car on Pearl Street, and Joe Romano parked his behind the hotel. With magnum in hand, I walked into the hotel through the front door, and Joe enters through the back door. We arrive in the bar at the exact same time, and we see one another. You want to talk about serendipity? What happened was very weird. I'm holding my magnum and I see Joe is holding a magnum as well! I said, 'What is this?' I point to my magnum and say, 'I bought this to celebrate my birthday with you guys.' Joe, excited, points to his and says, 'Me too! It's my birthday too! And I bought the same thing to celebrate with you guys!' Joe was two years my junior, but we were born on the same day. As close as we were, we never knew that about each other until that afternoon."

Sam was able to add a Sunday afternoon jam session. All seemed to be going well until one Saturday night when Tony paid Sam and abruptly said, "This is your last night. I'm making a change. I'm bringing in go-go girls. You guys are finished." Sam told him to wait a minute, how could he say they were finished, just like that? He told Tony that he had to give them two weeks' notice so they could find other work elsewhere. Tony said,

"Notice? There's no notice!" Sam accused him of being a prick. Briandi jumped over the bar and said, "You calling me a prick?!" Sam says, "I thought he was going to do me in, and I said, 'No, you're acting like one. When someone gets let go, you give 'em time to find something else.'" The Prince Edward gig ended, as did the Briandi-Noto friendship.

THE RENAISSANCE

After that fiasco, Frank St. George told Sam of a place up the street from the Prince Edward, a coffee house called The Boar's Head. Frank said, "It's kind of a hippie-beatnik type place that isn't doing very good. The owner fixed it up. It's nice. If you give him a thousand dollars for the work he's put into it you can have it. The rent is forty-five dollars a month." With that, Frank St. George took Sam Noto to see the place.

Sam says, "We went there, and I spoke to the owner. I loved it; all wood paneling, fireplace, tables, and chairs. The owner told me that for a thousand dollars it was mine; I could take over the rent. It was worth it, but I didn't have a thousand dollars, which was cheap for a place downtown, and there wasn't much to fix. I started scouting around. I talked to Louie Marinaccio, who told me that he would put some money up and be my partner. I got Louie and Lavon Cavanaugh, a waitress from Big Mother's, and Sam Perla, a lawyer and jazz fan. We decided to do a four-way partnership, with each putting in two hundred and fifty, and we'd have a joint, a jazz club. We talked about getting a beer and wine license. Lavon would take care of the kitchen. Louie would be at the door collecting money. Sam Perla would take care of any problems that existed. It seemed like a good idea. Truthfully? I didn't have two cents. I went to my mother-in-law and told her the whole story; that I was tired of the road, and that opening our own club was a good idea because of the interest and fan base the band had acquired. She said she would give me the two fifty. With her bread we purchased the Boar's Head. I came up with the Renaissance name, and Joe Marfoglio, a wonderful artist, painted the exterior sign. My group played from ten in the evening till two in the morning on Friday, Saturday, and Sunday. Then we were off an hour, and we'd play from three until six. Levon made breakfast, and people from bars were lined up trying to get in for eggs and whatever they wanted. I think we charged a buck or two admission to pay the band. It was working out great. Playing jazz with Joe Romano was some of the best musical years of my life. We hit it off. We were like hand and glove.

"I was in touch with Paul Fontaine, a trumpet player who lived in Boston, Massachusetts. I contacted a guy in Syracuse, and one in Rochester whose names I can't remember. We were going to start a chain of jazz clubs and keep upstate guys working. It was our plan. It didn't work, but we ended up with places of our own; some were short lived. Mine? I couldn't get a beer and wine license. Next door, in what was once the Eagles Auditorium, there was a religious place. At that time when you applied for a beer and wine license you needed permission and cooperation from nearby businesses or residents.

"The religious place closed at about nine o'clock in the evening. It was for kids, and the Renaissance wouldn't open till ten, so I thought it was no problem. But the Reverend there, Reverend Forbes, turned me down. I'll never forget him. He wanted to see me. I went to his office. The Reverend asked me if I wanted to serve alcohol, and I told him yes, that I was a musician who didn't want to be on the road, that I wanted to be with my family. He told me, 'Well, you could come and play for us. Jesus would like that.' I said, 'I don't know, does Jesus like Bebop?' I told him that I needed to generate more income, and the only way for me to do that would be for me to sell beer and wine. You can't make a profit on food alone."

Though the Renaissance was, by all accounts, nice and quaint and had great music, Sam's application for a beer and wine license was denied due to severe resistance. Sam says, "We went downhill. Restaurants, coffee houses lose their charm and before long they dwindle. The police were on my case. They said we were selling drugs and booze. I wasn't selling anything! We had whiskey in back, but it was for the band. People smoked stuff in the john. I couldn't control that. Narcs were there. I couldn't search everyone who entered. The cops checked cups for booze. I wasn't serving booze to anybody. People brought in little jars with whiskey. Again, I couldn't search those who did. I was in business. I was trying to keep the music, everything alive."

The Renaissance fell by the wayside; after living from 1966 to early 1967 it died. For Sam and the others that was the end. Sam says, "Later on, Reverend Forbes bought the property and razed it. It became a parking lot for his people. All in all, it was a great year. We were making it, barely, but I made enough to keep my family going. Ironically, Joe Romano, me, the group recorded every night. Louie Marinaccio's widow, Gail, must have every tape he ever recorded. Louie had an amazing amount of music from that era."

THE PALACE, CAR BATTERIES, AND TAXI CABS

On the evening of April 6, 1967, the end times came to the Palace Burlesk, that eminent post-Civil War edifice whose luminous exterior had sparkled across Shelton Square for decades. The moment marked the last time Sam Noto's trumpet would be heard there. Before its demolition to further Buffalo's Urban Renewal plan, manager Joe DiMartina hired two extra musicians. They were bassist Tom Azarello and the fleet-footed Ang Callea. At Sam's request, the musicians were going to celebrate the Palace Burlesk. Sam's already great band now had three horns and three rhythm pieces, and what a truly great band it was.

The following details of this historic musical event are taken from Buffalo Memories: Gone But Not Forgotten, a great book by the late George Kunz, a highly acclaimed Buffalo writer and historian.

It was a gala performance: all 720 seats had been sold long in advance, with big blocks of tickets bought by the Saturn and Buffalo Clubs. A tall doorman in blue uniform with gold braid and buttons presided at curbside, helping guests alight on to a red carpet which stretched on into the Palace. Long, shiny cars started arriving before eight; men in black tie, women wearing floor-length gowns. From outside the area, visitors traveled by chartered bus. Almost a thousand people squeezed into the high, narrow building.

Sam says, "It's 1967 and I'm in the same situation as before; no income and what to do? What to do? I was down about losing the Renaissance and now the Palace. I had to find work. I knew Louie Marino worked making car batteries at the Iroquois Battery factory. We met, and Louie told me he thought they were hiring. I went there and filled out an application and was hired to work five and a half days a week. There, when you made car batteries there was an incentive. If you've got one hundred percent, so many batteries, you get piecework for those over that. Nobody did it because you'd get maybe a nickel per battery. Maybe you got seventy percent. To keep my mind active, I went for the one hundred percent. By the time I got the hang of it, I'd get that after lunch, by about one thirty. We worked till four o'clock. I'd get the hundred percent going, I'd get my whole truckload with batteries done, and I'd go to the john, put my feet up in the locker room, and get some shuteye. The foreman comes in and says, 'What are you doing?' "

"I'm just taking a nap," I replied.

"You can't do that, you have to work."

I said, "Check my batteries, I got one hundred percent."

"What? Nobody gets—"

"I got one hundred percent, go check them," I said.

"He goes away, comes back and says, 'You got one hundred percent. Don't you want to make extra money?' I told him no, and he left, frustrated. I saved an hour for sleeping. I had that gig six, seven months, five and a half days for eighty-two dollars a week. That was bad. And I was depressed. I left there. My brother, Bill, was driving for City Service Taxi and told me he made pretty good tips. I started driving for City Service in the winter months going into 1968. I'd get up when it was dark, go to work, and when I came home it was dark again. I was doing 10-hour shifts, 12-hour shifts. And most people didn't tip, and, if they did, it was a buck or something. I took tranquilizers. I'd come home, take one, get on the couch, watch TV, and fall asleep. Everyone in my house was depressed. The taxi company fired me when I called the dispatcher a son-of-a-bitch over the intercom. He was putting me down, yelling at me. I said, 'Hey, listen, you son-of-a-bitch, you're talking to a man who's going to be—'

'Pull it into the garage!'

I was fired from that job."

OFF TO LAS VEGAS

"I was with Louie Marino at a coffee shop," Sam told me, "and he suggested that I go to Las Vegas to find work. I told him that I didn't know anyone there. 'Carl Fontana from Louisiana is there. I worked with Carl in the Kai Winding trombone thing. You know Carl, you played with him,' Louie said.

"So, I called the Las Vegas musician's union and asked for Carl Fontana's number. I called him. I said, 'Carl, how are things in Vegas?' He says, 'There's work here.' I told him I was thinking of coming out there and Carl told me that there were house bands everywhere and musician work all the time. He said, 'You should come out. In fact, I've got a five-week jazz gig at the Silver Slipper. If you want that, you can come and check it out.' I told him I'd take it. Then he told me he needed a saxophone player, and did I know anybody? I suggested Joe Romano, I told him we'd been working together for a year at my club. Carl said, 'If Joe wants it he's hired.' He told us to be there July first, that the gig started at two o'clock in the morning on July fifth, for five weeks. 'Then you can check out the gigs around here,' he said."

Sam says, "It was a great offer, and I talked to Arleen. I told her, 'I think maybe we ought to move to Las Vegas. I've got a jazz gig to go to and I'll check it out. I'll go alone and see what's going on. If I find it's a place for me to work, I'll fly you out with the kids.' Then I only had the three boys. My daughter, Jennifer, was born in Vegas. So that was it. We moved from our house on Prospect Avenue and stored our stuff. Arleen and the kids went to her parents' house in nearby Attica, New York, to their two-acre place with a man-made lake that my kids loved.

"Joe Romano picked me up in his old Porsche convertible. It wasn't in good shape, and every time we stopped for gas it just guzzled it up. It also sucked up vast amounts of oil. It took four days to get to Vegas—four fun-filled days. We had lots of laughs going across the country. We stopped at motels. If we stopped earlier than bedtime we'd bring the horns in and jam. It was airconditioned. Just as we're nearing Flagstaff, Arizona, we smell gasoline.

"Joe, do you smell gas?"

"Yeah, what the hell is that?"

"I'm getting a headache," I said. 'I'm getting dizzy."

"We stopped at a gas station. The motor was in the trunk. We lift it up, and the station attendant looks at us and says, 'Well, there it is. Gasoline is dripping from the carburetor onto the engine block, and fumes got into your car.' Joe asked him if he could fix it. The attendant said he'd have to send away for parts and that it would be maybe a day or two. I said, 'A day or two? We have to stay in a hotel and wait?' I knew nothing about cars, but I looked in the engine and saw that gasoline was leaking from a screw. I borrowed the attendant's screwdriver, tightened the screw, and the leaking stopped. I gave him back his screwdriver and said, 'C'mon Joe, let's go.' The guy probably wanted to choke me because he couldn't make a bunch of bread off us by sticking it up our you-know-what! Joe and I jumped in the car. It was dark now, pitch black. Around midnight we went over the Hoover Dam. By then it was pretty much an hour or so till Las Vegas. As we come over this ridge, there's Las Vegas, all lit up. Until then you couldn't see a thing. You could see on the horizon some kind of light, but once you're over that ridge you saw the whole valley and the lights. I never saw it before from that point at night. So, we drove. We went up a main road leading to The Strip. We were on Paradise near Flamingo Road, heading toward The Strip. It was about two o'clock in the morning. I said, 'Joe, we made it! Let's stop at this bar and have a drink.'

"We parked, entered the bar, and ordered cold beer and shots of vodka. Three others were there. Joe says, 'Hey Sam, see that guy across the bar? I think that's Red Rodney.' I look at the guy and he looks at us. Joe goes to him and waves to me, indicating that I should come to them. It was Red Rodney, who was a 'Bird' sideman. Red was with Herbie Phillips, another good jazz trumpet player, and a guy I didn't know. We're rapping, and I say we're doing the Silver Slipper gig with Carl Fontana. I say that I'm going to stay but that Joe is going back East after the gig. I said I was moving here and working in the hotels if possible and bringing my family out. Red Rodney says, 'Good, we'll come and see you at the Slipper.'

"We said goodbye and we left. I don't know why, but I decided to call Carl Fontana. Vegas is a twenty-four-hour town, so I figured he wouldn't mind. I called, and Carl told us to come on over. We went to his house for a taste and listened to Miles Davis records. Carl said that this was the kind of band he wanted, a real jazz band. I said, 'Carl, Joe and I have been playing together for a long time. We know exactly what each of us is doing. It should be okay, man.' "

Sam and Joe left Carl Fontana, and amid the Vegas hoopla they found a cheap motel near the Slipper. They checked in and crashed. In the morning, leaving for breakfast, they opened the door. The heat was awful. Sam says they almost passed out. After breakfast they picked up a six-pack of beer. Sam told me, "We didn't know that drinking beer or alcohol in this heat makes you dehydrate. We're chugging till gig time, 2:00 AM, so we had all night to screw around, but by two o'clock we were wiped out, dehydrated from all that drinking.

"Still, we were raring to go. Joe and I were playing and were up each other's wazoo; we were ripping it and feeling great. Fontana's looking at us with a look that says, 'What's going on here?' We get off after the first set, and musicians who come from work to hear us go up to Carl and say, 'Hey man, where did you get these fantastic guys?' Carl is getting accolades on our behalf, accolades he thought he should be getting. He and Gus Mancuso were supposed to be the main jazz guys in Vegas, but here come Noto and Romano.

"We did the gig, and soon after Carl was to leave for Los Angeles for two days on The Della Reese Show. Carl asked Joe if he could use the Porsche. Joe said he could, but he'd have to put oil in all the time because otherwise it would be screwed up. Carl said he'd take care of it. So, Carl leaves, and Joe and I played as a quintet. People loved us, and so did Cy Fenton, the pit boss who was Carl's good friend. We finished the gig. Later on, me, Joe and Cy went to the north part of town to a jam session. We're having a drink and Cy says, 'You guys sounded fantastic together.' Jokingly, Joe says, 'We don't need that Fontana guy.' We laughed about it."

Two days later, Joe Romano got a phone call from Carl Fontana. Returning from LA, Carl didn't put oil in the Porsche. The engine blew and there was a big hole in the block. Carl got a ride in and left the car in the desert. Joe was wigging out. Carl said, "Oh yeah, I'll help you pay for it, don't worry."

Sam says, "One of the guys in town drove us to the car and we had it towed. Joe lost all his bread. He had wanted to sell that car in Vegas, and though it needed work, it was a collector's item. Now it was junk. Carl never gave Joe a penny for that. But when Carl returned for the gig he got wind of Joe's 'we don't need that Fontana guy' remark. Suddenly Carl stops talking to me, but he's talking to Romano, who owned the remark. In spite of everything it was still fun, even though on and off the stand Carl was hostile to me. When he'd call a tune he'd say to Joe, 'Tell your friend next to you we're going to play Just Friends,' rather than saying, 'Let's play Just Friends.' I thought, 'Hey, fuck you, man.' What really got Carl mad was that Joe Romano and I went in there hot, real hot. He didn't expect that. He thought he was going to be the main guy, but people were wigging out over Joe and me, and I think that was the beginning. All he needed was one more thing to turn him against us, and Romano's remark to Cy Fenton was it. Carl got real spooky on me and fired us in the last week. He brought in Zoot Sims. Joe and I were screwed. Joe went back East, and I stayed.

"The word through the grapevine was about the big blown-out feud I had with Carl Fontana. It was taken way out of proportion on Carl's part and on others. I had nothing to do with it. Carl is accusing me of undermining his gig? What? I was thankful, happy to have the gig. Joe Romano was the one joking. We were wacked out, but evidently Cy Fenton, who heard Joe say it, took it seriously and told Carl.

"After that, I met Archie LeCoque, an old friend who was on Kenton's band throughout the Balboa fiasco, and who was in the

Flamingo Hotel house band. Archie said he had heard that I wanted to stay in Vegas. 'Is that true?' he asked. I told him, 'Yeah, but I got to put a card in and wait three months, right?' Archie promised to see what he could do. He said he would talk to Russ Black, the leader at the Flamingo, who wasn't happy with his first trumpet player.

"I met Russ Black. He took me to the union office, and because he was in dire need of a first trumpet player, he convinced them to hire me on the spot. Carl fires me, and suddenly I'm in the Flamingo show band in which Chico Alvarez is a member. At the time Chico was a Vegas musician union official, and about to quit playing. I remembered him from his Les Brown days, and I knew that, long before me, he was on Kenton's band. The Flamingo trumpet section at the first rehearsal was Chico, me, and Wes Hensel. Bill Harris, the great Jazz at the Philharmonic trombonist was on the band, as was trombonist Ray Sims (Zoot's brother), drummer Sandy Savino, Billy Chris on bass, alto Fred Haller, and baritone Kenny Hing, who was formerly with Basie. It was a good band with guys who've been around. It was fun, and I was there for a while, but it was shows. The first act I played when I got there was Sergio Franchi, the Italian singer.

"Immediately I searched for a three-bedroom apartment. I called Arleen and sent her money. She and the kids flew out. I bought a junk car for ninety bucks, picked them up at the airport, and went to the apartment. Me, Arleen, and my three sons started digging into Vegas. Later, I got Red Rodney on the Flamingo band to play third trumpet. One night, Red told me that he had a record date coming up in LA and wanted me to do it with him."

Sam Noto loved Red Rodney's playing. Alongside Dizzy, and Frank Navarro, Red was one of Sam's favorites. In Buffalo in the late 40s, a young Sam listened to Woody Herman records when Red and Gene Ammons were on the band. He loved their solos on "More Moon." Sam told me, "But when I got to know Red, I knew he had a problem with Truth."

Red said, "Sam, I want to do this Clifford Brown solo on 'Daahoud' as the head and then you'll play it."

"Yeah, yeah," said Sam.

"Can you get that solo?"

"I can get it."

"Red said, "You play the harmony and we'll rehearse.""

Sam told me that he knew this was nonsense. He really didn't feel like playing, but they went to reed man Jimmy Mulidore's place to listen to "Daahoud." Sam told me what happened next.

"We rehearsed all this stuff, and Red says, 'Don't forget, Monday, I'll pick you up and we'll drive to LA to record.' I told him, 'Okay, okay, sure Red.' The next morning at ten o'clock, I can't believe it, Arleen wakes me up and says, 'Red Rodney is waiting for you in his car.' "

Sam threw a few things together and got in Red Rodney's car. Red said, "We're going to LA to do the album. I got Dolo Coker on piano, Shelly Manne on drums, and Ray Brown on bass." Sam tells it. "We get there, and a couple of horns are needed for non-solo background. I got Larry Covelli on tenor, and Billy Byers on trombone. We do 'Daahoud' and we called it 'Superbop,' and that became the name of the album later released."

THE FLAMINGO HOTEL, A PAID VACATION, CHICKEN WINGS, AND JOE GUERCIO

Sam says, "Russ Black, the Flamingo leader, was a good guy, a good boss. I played for him for a whole year, and I got a two-week paid vacation. In my lifetime this was unheard of. I was making pretty good money; five hundred and fifty dollars a week. We were renting but living well, and Arleen was happy. After several months into the gig, I put away some bread and bought a brand-new Chevy station wagon for twenty-six hundred dollars from a guy in Flagstaff, Arizona, who drove it to Vegas. It was now 1969, and vacation time. I put the family in the wagon and we drove to Buffalo to visit the folks. We stayed at my in-laws' place. Later, we saw my parents. After that I met up with Larry Covelli and his wife, Carol. Arleen and I went to the Anchor Bar for dinner. We were sipping wine when Frank Bellisimo, the owner, came from the kitchen and said, 'Sam, I heard you guys were here. I thought you were in Las Vegas.' I said yeah, that we were here on vacation. Frank said, 'Wait a minute, I've got to show you something.' Frank went to the kitchen and came back with some chicken wings. We're sitting, looking at Frank, and I said, 'What's that?' Frank said, 'These are chicken wings. We do them a certain way, we just got into this.' I said, 'Chicken wings? My mother throws them out when she cooks chicken.' Frank took offense, but we ate a few wings and told him they were great. That was before the big craze with the whole original chicken wing. We stayed in the area for the two weeks. It really wasn't two weeks; we had to make allowances for the drive. So, we got in the car and took a leisurely trip to Vegas. We stayed in motels a few times and the kids went swimming; all that stuff."

Upon returning to Vegas, Sam returned to The Flamingo as well. He told me, "We had some of the better acts; Ella Fitzgerald, some pretty good singers, some comics, that Buffalo comic, he was pretty famous. What was his name…? Oh yeah, Dick Shawn. We played lots of big acts. The usual show biz stuff, and I was getting disillusioned again. After the gig we'd go to Roy Shaynes's house; he was the bass player. After playing two shows it's two in the morning, and we'd get wacked out and play. Roy's garage was converted into a studio and he recorded everything. I went there with Sandy Savino. Menza came by when he was in town. Everyone came there to play until sunrise, go home, sleep most of the day, and back to work. That's the only avenue we had to play jazz and keep what we had, our passion in line. Otherwise, it was redundant; shows, shows, and shows. And like I say, I was fed up with the whole thing and was drinking a lot more.

"There's no 'last call' in Vegas. You drink till you drop. It was getting out of hand. Russ Black and I got into a big hassle and we parted. Then the whole band got fired. Russ thought I was 'connected' and made that happen. I said, 'No Russ, where'd you hear that crap?'

"At the time, Tommy Perillo, a fine lead trumpeter for Joe Guercio at The Hilton, left for MGM. Guerico heard I wasn't working and offered me Perillo's chair. I accepted, and now I'm at The Hilton, but it's the same old thing; shows. I had to play Elvis's show, but he brought his own trumpet player. I thought, 'Oh boy, I'm getting four weeks off with pay.' Joe Guercio says, 'No, oh no. The other guy is getting off, you're playing second.' I said to Joe, 'What a drag man, the guy's taking the first trumpet's place. Why do I have to play second?' Joe said, 'That's it.' So, I got screwed.

"We played a lot of acts at The Hilton, and then, on my say so, we hired Charlie Davis, a really good high note trumpet player. I was getting older and figured I could use some help. So, Charlie came in. He was fine. I gave him some lead parts. Also on that band was James Moody. I couldn't believe it when I knew he was coming. One night I'm in the dressing room and I see Charlie Davis, and he's down in the mouth. I asked him what was wrong, and he told me he had gotten fired. I asked him why and he told me, 'Guercio's got this guy, Tony, coming in. I guess they think he can play higher than me.'

"I wigged out. I went to Guercio's dressing room and freaked out; 'Joe, why didn't you talk to me? I like Charlie. I like the way he plays. This other kid, I don't know who he is.' Guercio said, 'I heard about this guy and I'm hiring him.' I told him, 'I don't dig this at all, Joe! I'm supposed to be your first trumpet player. You should've talked to me, like any leader who's making big changes in any section!' I had a big scene with the one-time Black Rock piano player, and I quit. I was out of work for two weeks."

Sam went on, "Then I heard that Tommy Moses, the bandleader at the MGM, a brand-new hotel, wanted me to do the production show at the MGM; dancing girls and all that, like a variety show. I needed the gig. Billy Byers did the charts, and, knowing I wasn't working, recommended me. The band didn't play where the show was happening. We were in the basement, with no windows; a concrete block place. You came dressed as you liked, and they'd pipe the music onto the stage, and the conductor had a monitor to see what was going on. It was the most degrading gig I'd ever had. No rapport with the audience or the dancers; nothing. It was the worst. I didn't last long. I don't think I made two weeks. I made the opening show, and a few other nights till they got somebody, and I left. By then I was really bugged. I'm thinking I've got to leave Vegas. This is crazy."

Paul Grozny, a booking agent from Toronto, was in Vegas visiting a friend, Billy Chris, a bass player Sam knew from The Flamingo. Grozny knew of Sam from the Kenton and Basie bands. Billy and Grozny asked Sam to have a drink with them, and he did. Paul Grozny said, 'Sam, you know, there's a jazz club in Toronto that I book. It's called Basin Street. Would you like to play jazz music there for two weeks? I'll give you seven hundred and fifty dollars a week; your flight and your room are paid." Sam agreed to do it.

Sam flew to Toronto and stayed at a hotel near the gig where he played his jazz with a local rhythm section. It was Gary Williamson, and Dave Young on bass, and he had a marvelous time. He didn't know Guido Basso lived in Toronto—they were once together in Louie Bellson's big band. Sam says, "Guido's here and he's doing lots of studio work in town, and he came to see me. He said, 'Hey man, how you doing? Why don't you move to Toronto? We could use a guy like you. There's lots of work here. You'll do well. You'll play jingles, some variety shows, and TV work. And there's jazz clubs in town.' I said I'd think about it."

The Basin Street gig ended, and Sam returned to Vegas. He thought about what Guido had said. Then Tommy Moses called Sam and offered him a job at the MGM as the first trumpet; not beneath the hotel but in the MGM showroom. Sam took the gig. Tommy Perillo, the excellent first trumpet player who had left Joe Guercio's Hilton band for the MGM, had suggested him. Sam says, "I went to work for Moses, a real great guy from Chicago. That was a good band with a bunch of New York guys on it. I felt pretty good there. Moses was a good boss. We played the big stars; Dean Martin and others. It was a good gig, but I was still caught up in that show thing. I asked Arleen, 'What do you think of another move?' She said, 'What now?' I told her about Toronto. Arleen said, 'What? Toronto? Are you crazy? We're going to get cold weather again? We went through all of that crap!' We decided to do it because we'd be close to Buffalo, the folks, and friends."

THE MOVE TO TORONTO

In 1975, Sam was in Vegas before leaving the MGM and moving to Toronto. They finished a show and heard there would be some kind of music at a place on Paradise Road. Sam told me, "So I went there. I enter and see two people at this long bar. I see the back of a big, burly guy, and immediately I know it's Carl Fontana. There were some things bugging me about him. I was going to confront him, to explain that there was a misunderstanding about our Silver Slipper situation of long ago. I stopped behind him and said, 'Hey Carl.' He turned, and before I could say another word, he sucker punched me right in the mouth; right in the chops. I said, 'What the fuck?' The guy with Carl pulls him back and Carl says to me, 'C'mon, c'mon, what are you going to do?' I looked at him. By then my chops were swelling up. I said, 'Fuck you,' and walked to the other side of the bar. The bartender asked me if I was okay, and I said I was and ordered a cognac. He said, 'You want me to call the cops on this prick? I don't like that kind of stuff in here.' I said, 'No, fuck him. No cops. I know the guy. There's a bullshit story in his mind and it's closed. There's no talking to him.' I sat and drank. A girl who went with a friend of mine came over and said, 'Sam, are you okay? What was that all about?' I told her it was a long story, and I didn't want to get into it. We talked a bit and she left. After another cognac I left. I had to pass Fontana on the way out, and as I do, he turned to me and assumed a fighting position. I thought, 'What's wrong with this guy? His name is Fontana, a Sicilian from Baton Rouge,

Louisiana, but he didn't know anything about being Sicilian like West Side guys from Buffalo. I guess Southern Italians from Louisiana are different from us.'

"Years later, while living in Toronto, I had a gig at the Royal Hotel that ended early. I heard Carl Fontana was playing at Bourbon Street with a local rhythm section so, even after all that Vegas bullshit with him, I thought I'd stop for a drink before going home. I went there, and it was crowded. Carl was on the stand. When he got off, someone approached him and pointed to me. Evidently, he's saying, 'Sam Noto is here.' Carl came over. He said, 'How are you doing, Sam?' I said, 'Fine, Carl, how are you doing?' He said, 'You know, we ought to forget all about that Vegas stuff.' I said, 'You started that. Joe and I were having a good time when you left for California. That's all I know. We were smashed, making a joke with Cy Fenton, and you took it all wrong.' Carl said, 'Well, I'd like to forget about it.' I said, 'Okay, Carl, good enough.' Carl said, 'Will you have a drink with me?' I said, 'No,' and walked away."

OH, CANADA

At the Canadian Consulate, Sam and Arleen acquired applications to enter Canada. It was painstaking. The authorities had to learn everything about them. Sam and Arleen filled pages with words. Sam was busted in Vegas once for DUI and for possessing pot, and thought he'd be denied entrance. They sent in the applications and waited to be checked out.

Nine months elapsed. Sam was at the MGM when the okay came. They had to get American passports to cross the border in Buffalo to get to Toronto on April first. April Fool's Day! Sam says, "I quit the MGM. I told them it was great working there, but I'm making a move and leaving Vegas. On my last night they had a party for me. They took a collection, some bread for the trip back. We sold our four-bedroom house in the valley that I bought for twenty-eight thousand when I was doing well in the latter part of the Flamingo gig. It had a two-car garage and was brand-new, never lived in. Would you believe that? My mortgage was two hundred and forty-five dollars a month, including insurance, and no taxes. There were none in Nevada. I had a brand-new house for two hundred and forty-five dollars a month! That was 1975. We sold it for thirty-three thousand. Now homes in that area sell for three hundred thousand. Believe this?! That's my big decision making. #@$%&#%%$!!! Right? North American Movers came, took our stuff, and would deliver it to Toronto. We jumped in the car and started our journey. Our daughter Jennifer, who was born in 1972, was with us. Today she is Jennifer Noto Greene and lives in Buffalo with her husband and our three beautiful grandchildren.

"The move is happening with baby Jennifer and two sons. Michael, the oldest of three sons, stayed in Vegas where he had many friends and liked his job. Once home, we stopped to see Arleen's parents. We had to cross the bridge on April first. We get there, and due to a severe snowstorm, it's closed, as is the highway to Canada—the Queen Elizabeth Way. No traffic; the storm was that bad. We turned around, returned to my in-laws, and stayed there a few days till the weather blew over."

On April fourth when they returned to the Peace Bridge, an authority figure told them, "You were supposed to be here on the first." Sam said to him, "Are you kidding? Look at your records, the bridge was closed that day, and so was the QEW." The authorities hemmed and hawed, but finally let the Notos through.

They had a house in Toronto to which they could go. Tenor sax Pat LaBarbara, originally from the Rochester, New York area, lived in Toronto. Sam called him, and Pat found a three-bedroom house for them in Etobicoke. The rent was three hundred and ninety-five dollars a month. By today's standards, it was inexpensive. Sam says, "We're waiting and waiting for the movers. We called North American Movers and found out that during the snowstorm they had dropped our furniture and stuff in Buffalo! I complained, 'You were supposed to bring our stuff to Toronto; I paid for all the way to that city!' The North American rep says, 'The driver had other deliveries for other people, so he dropped your stuff off at some storage place in Buffalo.' I went nuts! I called Joe Carlisi and told him. He said, 'Sam, check into a motel. I'll get you reimbursed. You can't stay there with no furniture, no beds or nothing.'

"We checked in at a Holiday Inn in downtown Toronto. Joe Carlisi got in touch with North American Movers, reamed on them, and they paid for the three, four days it took to bring our furniture up. They paid for the hotel and gave me food money. Joe, a lawyer, did me a real big favor. Otherwise we'd have been stranded and sleeping on the floor. Anyway, we moved in, and I'm in touch with Paul Grozny, who had previously hired me for the Basin Street gig. He says, 'Sam, I'll put you in there again for two weeks, so you'll have something when you're here.'

"Finally, the furniture came, and we settled in to that house on Prince Edward Drive. Of all the names—it was the same as the hotel in Buffalo. It was a nice little house. It was good that Paul Grozny put me to work when I arrived. Many musicians went to jazz clubs after their gigs to check out the players, usually an American with a local rhythm section, and that's what I was. Zoot Sims, Paul Desmond, Al Cohn, Tom Harrell, and other big guys, great musicians played there. And the local players were great as well. I'm playing, and Guido Basso came in. Guido says, 'Sam, I'm glad you made it. I'll throw some work your way.' The great lead trumpet player, Arnie Chyoski, came in and introduced himself. A lot of musicians did, and fortunately, they were impressed. Jazz-wise, I was pretty much at the top of my game, so I could showcase myself to start freelancing. That was most of the work there."

TORONTO, ONTARIO

Early in 1978, while living in Toronto, Sam received a phone call from Don Schlitten who owned Xanadu records, and for whom Sam recorded. Schlitten was getting several of his label's artists to play the Montreux Jazz Festival in Geneva, Switzerland. He told Sam to meet the group in New York and said, "From there we'll fly out on Swiss Air for the festival. We'll have one day off to get it all together, do the gig, and come home."

Sam flew to New York and met everyone in an airport conference room at JFK. Present were Sam Most, flute; Ron Cuber, baritone sax; and tenor players Al Cohn and Billy Mitchell. Sam says, "The rhythm section was two piano men; Dolo Coker and Barry Harris. There was a guitar, bass, and a good drummer, a dude from Los Angeles. We got there and discussed what to do. I pretty much played with Ron Cuber, a great baritone player. Everything was recorded, and we were paid. Al Cohn and I got to be pretty tight. Everyone flew from New York to Switzerland for the festival. Al Cohn sat next to me on the plane. The airline gave you a martini with dinner. I had filet mignon, salad, red wine, and cognac. The food was fantastic."

After dinner Sam and Al were drinking at a good pace, but soon their conversation faded. Al Cohn was smashed, and in the parlance of the jazz set, he was "out of it." The lights were dimming. People on the plane were sleeping, and others were attempting to do so. Sam says, "Al Cohn only had one eye, and it was open. A stewardess came by and I asked her, 'Can you bring us another cognac?' She said, 'Are you kidding?' She looked long and hard at the wasted Al Cohn and said, 'Your friend, are you sure he wants one?' I said, 'Oh yeah, he does.' She said, 'He certainly doesn't look like it.' I looked at the sleeping Al and told her, 'He has a bad eye.' She gave me a strange look, left, and came back with cognac. 'These are on me,' she said.

"It's early morning. The plane lands and soon the group are on the ground. I saw a bar. I wanted another cognac. I turned and saw Barry Harris and another musician carrying Al Cohn off the plane. They walked by the bar where I'm drinking. Barry Harris stopped, looked at me and said, 'You've got to be kidding me!' The next day at the hotel we're having an outdoor breakfast and here comes Al Cohn. I ask him, 'How do you feel, man?' He says, 'Like a million lira.' I said, 'That's not too much bread.' Al and I were pretty tight. Later he played at my club in Buffalo."

DON SCHLITTEN AND XANADU RECORDS

Don Schlitten called Sam again in the summer of 1978. He offered to fly Sam to New York to do an album. Sam agreed. Don gave Sam the name of a studio in the RCA building and told him the gig would last about six hours and pay seven hundred and fifty dollars. Sam asked him, "Who's on this thing?" Schlitten said, "I'm not telling you anything, just be there, okay?"

Sam flew to New York. He arrived at the studio, walked in, and saw Blue Mitchell, the great trumpet man sitting on a chair, warming up. Sam introduced himself and said to Blue Mitchell, "I must be in the wrong studio." A voice from the engineer's booth said, "No Sam, it's the right studio." It was Don Schlitten. Sam says, "I'm thinking, what's going on? As Blue and I rap, my buddy Al Cohn enters with an entourage. I look and see another great tenor man, Dexter Gordon, with pianist Barry Harris, drummer Freddie Wade, and Sam Jones, and I'm still thinking, 'What's going on?' Schlitten leaves the booth and says, 'I want you guys to have a jam session. I'm recording it and putting it out.' So, we talked about what to play. I suggested 'Half Nelson.' Blue and I could play the Charlie Parker chart, and the saxes could play melody. We played our hearts out for the required six hours. It truly was a jam session, a classic that came out beautifully."

In the fall of 1978, Schlitten called Sam for the third time. He wanted Sam to come to California, to LA, to do an album under Sam's own name, and later be a sideman on one for piano man Kenny Drew. Sam said yes. Schlitten sent him a plane ticket and

Sam flew to LA. Sam says, "Menza and Rose (Menza's wife) met me at the airport and I stayed with them for a day. The recording studio was in an ocean resort south of Los Angeles. Venice comes to mind. It was one of those quaint little towns on the ocean where people roller skate on the boardwalk; a real California place, and it was beautiful. Larry Covelli drove me to the studio. The first day of recording I had Sam Most on flute, Monty Budwig on bass, and Frank Butler on drums. It was a strange combination, but it came off well. We did it in six hours. We drove back to LA and hung out at Menza's for great food and, as usual, a drinking session. We laughed about the old days. The next day at that studio I played on Kenny Drew's album with Leroy Vinegar on bass and Charles McPherson on saxophone. I've learned that Japan now owns the rights to those Xanadu recordings. They're considered collectible and are being sold for lots of money. I called Don Schlitten. I said, 'Don, I saw on the Internet that the Japanese are selling all the Xanadu albums.' He said, 'Yes, correct. I sold them the rights.' I said, 'Shouldn't I see some bread since I put all of my compositions through you?' He agreed I should. He quickly changed the subject and said, 'Sam, if you need some records, I'll send you a box of acetates.' Though he didn't say it, it was the usual; one dog, one bone, and fuck you! I very much appreciate that he recorded me several times and I got to do what I do—write music and play it. But my passion, the music I wrote and played, is sold world-wide and I get nothing. Survival is difficult when you're treated unfairly."

After recording the albums, Don Schlitten booked Sam, Dolo Coker, Sam Most, Monty Budwig, and Frank Butler for a two-night gig at Donte's, a small but famous jazz club in North Hollywood. Sam says, "Opening night the place was packed. Everyone in LA who once lived in Buffalo was there. I'm on the bandstand for the first set. At a table in front of me are Dizzy Gillespie and Leonard Feather, the jazz critic for Down Beat Magazine. Dizzy waved to acknowledge me. After the set we spoke. He introduced me to Leonard Feather. Dizzy said, 'I got in the cab at the airport and asked the driver if he knew where Donte's was. He said he did. I asked if he knew who was playing there and he said yeah, that it was Sam Noto and Sam Most. I said, 'Sam Noto? Drive me there.' '

"Needless to say, I was nervous because Dizzy was there. He was a beautiful cat. We always got along whenever our paths crossed. That night he dug what I did. The next day in a local newspaper I read Leonard Feather's review of the band. 'Given the opportunity to play jazz music every night, Sam Noto could be a big force in the music.' That's all he said. I read that, and I didn't know what to make of it. I felt he didn't say whether he liked it or not. Someone who read it said, 'Coming from Leonard Feather, it's a good review.'

"Donte's was a great gig on and off the stand, because all the Buffalo guys at the bar would wait for me and we'd drink and have laughs. When the gig ended, the musicians met individually with the owner in the kitchen to be paid. What little we made was to sweeten Schlitter's record deal. The owner sees me and takes out his paperwork. I knew I bought some drinks and knew I had a tab. I asked him if we were straightened out. He says, 'Yeah, I've got it here, you owe seventy bucks.' I said, 'What?!' He says, 'Your tab surpassed what you earned.' I went back to the bar and hung out with the guys, who later drove me to the airport, and I left for Toronto."

DON MENZA

Sam was freelancing when Menza called from California to say he had a month-long gig at the Riviera in Las Vegas with drummer Louie Bellson. Menza said, "We'll be the opening act for Wayne 'Neuter,' ha-ha, Newton, and it pays pretty good." Sam recalls, "I don't remember how much it paid but he was right, it was good bread. We stayed at the Riviera and played only for the opening act. That was about twenty minutes. Louie Bellson hired Menza, me, John Hurd on bass, and Frank Collette on piano. Menza drove in from LA and we played the big band charts using the Riviera house band. I got out there, we rehearsed, and it was a sweet gig. Louie Bellson said, 'While we're in Vegas we're doing an album with you guys and a local Congo drummer.' We went in the studio and did an album called Sidetrack. It's since been released and it's excellent. I didn't think so at the time because in the studio while we were playing I'm thinking we're getting nothing back. I never liked playing with earphones. I don't think I get the full perspective. Besides not liking that, it was a real hard studio too. It was dead. You didn't hear the full sound, and Louie was in a completely different room with the Congo drummer. We saw him through a window. When we finished recording, we're in Menza's car driving to the Riviera, and I asked him to take me to Lake Mead because I wanted to jump in. I was thinking it was that bad a record. Menza said, 'Why, what do you mean? It sounded good to me, but it was funny playing in that studio.' We both thought it was hard to play in there, but we didn't think about it anymore. It was extra bread. They sent the recording tapes to a young mixer in San Francisco."

While they were doing the gig, Joe Romano was living in Vegas. Sam was hanging with Joe in the daytime, and at night, with Menza, he would go to the gig. Sam had lived in Vegas for seven years and knew many musicians. Then there were some after-hours jam sessions, and Sam and Menza played. Joe "Mouse" Bonati was in town. Sam says, "He came in, checked us out, as did piano man Gus Mancuso. One night between the shows I'm at the slots in the casino and over the intercom I hear, 'A long distance telephone call for Sam Noto.' I pick up the house phone. An operator says, 'You have a call from Arleen Noto in Toronto.' When Arleen came on the phone I said, 'What's wrong, what's wrong?' She said, 'Your son, Chris, had a date and he wanted to use the car so I let him. He went to see a movie at a drive-in but evidently, he bought some booze and was drinking there. While driving home after the movie he smacked into a house.' I said, 'Oh my God, is he okay?' Arleen said, 'Oh yeah, he's fine, but the car is totaled.' It was a brand-new Ford. I was glad to hear no one got hurt, but when I got back to Toronto I went through that thing of finding a new car. So, then I'm making payments on the shattered Ford and on its replacement.

"After the gig, Wayne Newton had a party on his ranch in Vegas. He invited Louie Bellson and our guys. Menza had to get back, so he left. I asked Louie if I could bring Joe Romano since Don wouldn't be there. Joe picked me up at the Riviera and we drove to Newton's ranch. There was a big gate and you pushed a button and let them know who you were. I said, 'It's Sam Noto and Don Menza.' The gate opened, and we drove past all these animals and a great house with an eight-car garage loaded with vintage autos. The party was outdoors, so we never got to see the inside of the house. We were never invited in, even to show it off. We're sitting under trees, and there's a bar with a bartender, so we're having a few drinks. Pearl Bailey, Louie Bellson's wife, was there. Wayne Newton invited a lot of people. Joe said, 'Sam, this is great.' Then we see a few guys pushing this huge covered smoking rotisserie. I told Joe, there's probably filet mignons or lobster in there. Joe and I watched as they put the rotisserie in place, lifted the hood, and told everyone to form a line at your leisure, and partake. Joe and I went up there. We saw the contents and looked at each other in amazement. We couldn't believe it! Wayne Newton served hamburgers and hot dogs to his guests! We thought there'd be exotic food. We laughed about that for a year. Newton was a multi-millionaire. You could tell by the surroundings. He worked in Vegas all the time, and for a lot of bread. Each night at the end of the show, Newton, who was a drummer, had a drum battle with Louie Bellson."

Sam left Vegas and went home to see Don Menza, who was in Buffalo. They visited Steve Willis, a trumpet player who lived on Lake Erie in a home he was refurbishing, and where a party with many people was in progress. Willis, a college professor, would soon conduct a Buffalo Philharmonic Orchestra concert with Menza and strings on Willis's arrangement of a Stan Getz tune. Menza would play the first part of the concert with the BPO, and Sam would join him later in a quintet setting to play charts written by a Niagara Falls piano player. Sam says, "It was a great party. Dick Fadale and his kids were there, as were my daughter and Arleen, who swam in the lake. There was plenty of booze and food. When we get there, I hear this band playing, and I'm listening. I knock on the door where the music is coming from. Someone opened it. Menza, who was in the room, saw me and told me to come in. He said, 'Wait till you hear this!' He had Sidetrack, the mixed Vegas album we did with Bellson, and he was playing it for Fadale and Willis. I couldn't believe it! The mixer in San Francisco did a fantastic job. It's great. The frame was excellent, and everything I worried about was entirely missing. It was one of the better small band albums Louie Bellson ever made. Even reviewers said that. You never know. Initially I was depressed about that session, but when I heard what we did, I was happy.

"Another time while I'm living in Toronto, Menza's there for a gig at Bourbon Street with a local rhythm section. He calls me and says, 'Are you busy on such and such a week?' I said I wasn't and he said, 'Well, if you can work for scale like the others, you can work with me at Bourbon Street. We won't use a piano, just you, me, Clark Terry, and Dave Young.' I said it sounded okay to me, and Menza said, 'Great! The CBC, the Canadian Broadcasting Company, will put a truck in the alley behind the club to record us.'

"We went there, me and Menza with his tape recorder. The CBC's truck with mikes was set up and we played and recorded three of the six nights. But Menza recorded every night. We played some of my charts and some of his. Menza said the band was burning! Many people heard those tapes and wigged out. Menza knew a producer in Spain who was interested in buying them and releasing them on a CD. In that case, we'd see some extra bread. The CBC gave the local guys and Menza some extra bread for the recording. It was on one of their coast-to-coast jazz shows. But it was never produced as a record. Menza and I had a great time with that. I'd pick him up, and he'd come to the house and have dinner. I had a Volkswagen. One time when I was making a turn Menza said, 'What's that noise?' I said, 'What noise? What are you talking about?' He said, 'That scraping.' He saw a Volkswagen dealership and told me to pull in. He goes in and buys brake shoes. While Arleen is cooking dinner for us I'm sitting with Menza outdoors having a beer, and he's putting brake shoes on my car. I'm telling you, this guy's nuts! He's great at it. We laughed about that for a long time."

Sam Noto went on to tell me, "There were many jazz clubs in Toronto while I was there. I remember a place around Yorkville; a hoity-toity area. It may have been called Blondies, I'm not sure. But Guido Basso and I, along with two trumpets and a rhythm section, rehearsed some stuff and went in there for a week and we were playing good. Guido told me, 'Jazz makes me nervous.' When he played jazz in the studios he wouldn't solo while recording. He'd go in on his own the next day and overdub his solo. I couldn't understand that. I wouldn't do that, you're missing the whole point of interacting with the band, but he was good at it and did it well. When we'd get ready to play the gig he'd say, 'Man, I'm nervous.' I'd say, 'What's there to be nervous about? Just have some fun. Play the way you play.' On our third night Guido got really nervous when Clark Terry, the great trumpet player, came in and sat at a front table. It was like Guido didn't know what to do. I said, 'Guido, just play man, just play.' So, we did, and when we finished, Clark invited us to his table to say how much he dug it. We had a good time with him."

ROB McCONNELL'S BOSS BRASS

Sam says, "After a few nights at that club Rob McConnell came in. He listened to a set and invited me to join him for a drink. He said, 'Hey man, you sounded fantastic. I've got a band here. I'd like you to play on my band.' I asked what kind of band it was, and he said it was a big band called Boss Brass. I said, 'Are you firing someone to hire me? If you are, I don't want enemies, word gets around. If that's the case I'll cool it.' Rob said, 'No, no, I'll add you. I have four trumpets, but I'll make it five. You'll get work, recordings.'"

Sam agreed to join the Boss Brass. He needed to make friends so as to work. He finished the gig with Guido, and after joining McConnell he started getting phone calls. At first it was a few casuals, and then some "jingle" work. Sam told me, "You do one of those for an hour and you get residuals. I started doing TV shows and getting in with the upper clique doing all the work. Arnie Chycoski liked me, as did Al Stanwyck, who also played lead. I was in that kind of clique too. I was starting to do well. My first gig with Rob McConnell was at Ontario Place, and he didn't have a fifth trumpet book. So, I'm sitting with no music in front of me and Al or Arnie would point and say, 'Here, play this.' So, I'd play from their chart. And then, 'Play this over here, take the solo there.' I was like a utility man, so to speak. When Rob started writing for five trumpets Al Stanwyck left the band, so there was Arnie, myself, Guido, Dave Woods, and Eric Traugott. So, Rob set me on second and third trumpet and would write solos for me on the third trumpet part. He'd have my name on the part, and everyone knew that was my chart. It got to be a lot of fun. Rob never recorded a jazz album. He'd get a lot of TV show openings, and he did a lot of that, but that was before I was there. As soon as I joined the band, that changed. Suddenly there was a 'hot' trumpet player. Guido soloed mostly on flugelhorn. I was the hot guy and Guido was the other guy. It seemed to work out. Rob started writing some good stuff. He was a great writer and a good arranger. He said we were doing an album on which I had some solos. I played 'My Man Bill' and he called it The Jazz Album, because all the others were big band things not associated with jazz. The Jazz Album was pretty good. We made several more. We made that digital, a direct to disc album. That was hard, because you had to play the whole side, finish, and you'd have ten seconds to get the next music up and start again. It wasn't like you do a take and listen to it and see if you like it or not. You had to do the whole side of the record because it went direct to disc. And then the disc was sent to Germany for processing. We did several albums. The band got to be pretty hot. We didn't work that often, but when we did they were good paying gigs. I was in on the cliques, and my bandmates who had jingles and things going with companies were hiring me and telling others to do so. I got into it, and I was doing well.

"Rob McConnell's band was getting booked in little towns around Ontario. We even did Art Park in Lewiston, New York. That gig paid well; actually, most of them did. If we traveled by bus, a caterer filled it with all kinds of food and booze. It was like a party, and when we got to the gig we felt great, and the band sounded wonderful. To play with that band was fun and musically challenging. The musicianship was outstanding. I've played with great lead trumpet players in big name bands all over the country, and Arnie Chycoski in Toronto was a monster first trumpet player. And Guido Basso is a great jazz player, as were Moe Kaufman, Eugene Amaro, and Ian McDougal. They were on the band. That's why it always sounded so good. Those guys were top-notch musicians. Some were great writers as well, like tenor man Rick Wilkins. That thing I recorded live at El Mocambo, 'I Love You,' was to be called 'Sam's Song.' Ian McDougal wrote it for me as a feature tune. But there was another tune with that title and it couldn't be used, so he called it, 'I Love You.' It was a really talented band.

"We went to California, I think that was 1982. We were to play four nights at Carmelo's, do the Monterey Jazz Festival near San Francisco, and jazz clinics at some of the schools. We were booked so solid we didn't have time to relax. We did the Monterey Festival and that went well. I soloed all over the place, and Arnie was popping away, playing all his stuff. Then we did the clinics, and on to Carmelo's for a straight-ahead jazz gig. Lots of people came to hear us, including all the Tonight Show guys; John Audino, Conte Candoli, Bill Perkins, Chris Lieb, and others. The band was really cooking. The local guys were feeding us a lot of things, presents, so to speak. You know what I mean. That was going on then in California.

"We were playing great, and the third night before the gig I went to Menza's home for dinner. I looked at my watch, oh man, before I knew it, it was ten minutes to nine. I said, 'Menza, I start at nine, drive me there.' Menza said, 'They're cool.' I said, 'No man, you don't know Rob. Get me there, please!' He drives, and I'm ten, fifteen minutes late. Everyone is on the bandstand, and they haven't played yet. Standing, arms folded and facing the audience, is Rob McConnell. Chuck Piscatello, who with his brother owned the place, stops me. 'Hey Sam, what's happening?' I said, 'What's going on?' He says, 'They haven't played yet.' I ask why not. Why didn't they start? Chuck says, 'Evidently, you weren't there.' I said, 'Well I better get up there, Rob is giving me daggers.' Chuck says, 'Come in the kitchen with me.' I said, 'Chuck, I've got to get on the stand.' He says, 'Hey man, it's my club.' We went into the kitchen and he gave me a little toot. I leave to go on the stand. All the guys are quiet, and Rob is staring at me. I say, 'I'm sorry, I got hung up.' Rob didn't say a word. The first tune he calls is 'Mrs. Beanheart,' a chart in which I play this tremendously hard passage, and then the solo. Rob figured I'd fall flat on my face since I hadn't warmed up. He had a vindictive streak. He took everything you did personally, like my being late. He was screwed up. I tried telling Menza, but he was 'No man.' Anyway, Rob calls 'Mrs. Beanheart' and goes, 'One, two, one, two, three, four,' and we're into this fantastic fast tempo. I play in unison with the flute, and then the hard passage I mentioned. A trombone solos briefly. My balls are breaking because he did this to me. So, I stand and start playing, and I'm coming in on a high F, and I kept coming down dramatically and kept going out. Everyone at the bar roared. They're screaming. I played the solo wacked out. But I was on the case, or as they say, 'in the moment.' The tune ended and the place erupted. They went berserk. Now Rob is more burned up. He evidently wanted to see me go down. I don't know what the hell was going through his mind. Anyway, the place was all, 'The band, the band!' Then Rob calls 'I hear a Rhapsody,' a soft slow ballad featuring an alto sax. But the audience is noisy. Rob stops the band, and the alto player sits. Rob folds his arms again and stares at the audience. Here's all these top-notch LA musicians, all these heavies, and they're like, 'What the fuck is going on? Who is this guy?' Rob waited for them to finally get quiet and starts the tune again. He had his quirks so to speak, and he had his ego, too—a big one.

"After California the band flew to Toronto, but I stayed behind. I went to Vegas for some extra work, a recording with a young trumpet player who wanted me there. There were a lot of ringers on that session; trumpet man Carl Saunders, Chuck Finley's brother, and Vinnie Tano, who was living in Vegas. After the session I visited my son, who still lived there, and then I hopped a plane to Menza's home in LA to rehearse for another album we were planning to do at Carmelo's. This would be the second one, the one with Frank Strazzeri, Shelly Manne, Sal Nistico, Menza, Andy Simpkins, and me. It's the one recently released. We rehearsed and went into Carmelo's for several nights with the recording truck outside. That's the album where I play 'These Are the Things I Love,' and 'Tenor Madness,' and everything Menza and Frank Strazzeri wrote. It was a great date."

RENAISSANCE II

Early in 1982 Sam Noto purchased Frank's Casa Nova on Bailey Avenue and East Ferry Streets on Buffalo's East Side. It was an old and long-time strip club of a different era, but Sam thought it would be a good jazz venue. Wanting it to reflect his 1960s Pearl Street mission, he called it the Renaissance II. He aspired to fill it with jazz super stars that he would import, but Sam, not having lived in Buffalo for a long time, didn't know that the area had changed dramatically. Owing to Buffalo's then political and socio-economic climate, Sam learned after the purchase that the venue was off limits and was perceived to be in a high crime rate area. That may be partially true—but everything about the situation, the purchase of the space, its intended purpose—was blown out of proportion with extensive and ignorant political nonsense emanating from City Hall.

Certain elected officials said that a jazz club would bring unsavory people to the neighborhood. That was a huge sore spot with Sam. Finally, permission to open was granted. The operation would be a family thing, worked by Sam and his sons. Sam says, "I had some great musical moments there. Tom Harrell, Don Menza, Scott Hamilton, and Chet Baker played in that room and made great music. Chet Baker sounded fantastic. He came in town without a trumpet. He asked me, 'Sam, what kind of horn are you using?' At the time, I was using a Bach Stradivarius with a 72 bell. I told him that. Chet said, 'Can I use it?' I said, 'You don't have a horn?' Chet said he didn't. I asked him if he had a mouthpiece.

Chet did. At the start of Chet's four days, a ritual occurred. Chet entered the club and from my office I hand him my beautiful Bach Stradivarius. Chet loved that horn. At night's end I took it back. Oh, did he play that horn! It was a good one and he loved it. So much so that I told the waitresses to keep an eye on it! That's the horn I used on 'These Are the Things I Love,' on Menza's second album. It had many colors to it. I put air in it in a different way. It responded beautifully. It was a great horn. I don't know why I got rid of it. I must have been in one of my dumb, off-balanced moods. Chet Baker? He brought people in, especially those who were afraid to frequent a venue in an area deemed to be off-limits. While Chet was there he recorded an album; Live at the Renaissance. Today it's collectible."

Also, in 1982, Jack Downes, a local entrepreneurial businessman, and this writer produced a successful fundraiser at Renaissance II for Sam Noto's one-time musical soul mate, Joe (Mouse) Bonati, who was stricken with cancer. Bonati and his wife came from Vegas for the event. Jazz musicians Bobby Militello, C.Q. Price, Elvin Shepard, and numerous others performed. Sam Noto's star-filled big band, one that rivalled any famous orchestra, brought down the packed house. However; for reasons stated earlier, Renaissance II failed. A quiet Sam Noto said, "It was a complete flop, and I walked away from another depressing aspect of my life."

The brilliant writer George Frazier, in depicting Nick's, the Greenwich Village jazz haunt of the 1930s and 40s wrote,

"But there are still those of us who... in days to come will think of it and be stabbed, not with any fake emotion, but with a genuinely heart-breaking nostalgia. We will think of that place, and all of a sudden the fragrant past... will sneak up on us and for a little while we will all be the sad young men."

George Frazier could have been writing about the many smoke-filled jazz watering holes that filled the corners of Buffalo's streets. Think Bafo's, Renaissance I, or the late dusky nights at the ill-fated Renaissance II per Chet Baker, Jazz's Prince of Darkness; The Young Man Without a Horn.

TORONTO, AGAIN

Sam returned to Toronto again and worked at the Royal York
Hotel, and once again he was playing for shows. Toronto was
extremely expensive. Sam and Arleen decided to move to Fort
Erie, a small Canadian town across the Niagara River from
Buffalo. Sam gives great thanks to Canada's medical benefit
system. He had knee surgery and gall bladder surgery, services he
could never have afforded in the States. Sam says, "If I were in the
States with those problems, I'd be dead. There's no way we're
leaving this country. Fort Erie is a nice, quiet town with few
problems. No big traffic jams, nothing. We were across the
Niagara River from Buffalo where our parents still lived, and we
could shoot across the Peace Bridge to see them. I was getting gigs
in my former home town. One was with Ang Callea in the pit at
Shea's Buffalo. That move to Fort Erie seemed like the right thing
to do."

For several years Sam drove to Toronto when called for
certain things. "No problem," he'd say to the callers. "It's only
ninety minutes." In time it became risky, but even so, for Sam it
was worth it. Up north he had a great quintet with Kirk McDonald,
Bob McClaren, Mark Eisenman, and Steve Wallace, and they
worked quite a bit. Sam was approaching his sixtieth year, and
driving to and fro was daunting, especially in winter. He knew the
lifestyle was turning stale. Sam told me, "It was too much, so,
while I'm gigging somewhat in Buffalo, I applied for Social
Security and my musician's union pension, which wasn't a big

deal. Then I told Rob McConnell to replace me and he did, with John McCloud, a fine player."

In late 1988 or 89 Sam received a call for his group to play in Toronto at the DuMaurier Jazz Festival. This was a televised outdoor event staged in a Toronto parking lot. A bandstand was set up. A few people were there. Chairs were supplied to create a concert atmosphere.

It was a great gig, one that he and his musicians felt good about. After the concert Sam was interviewed; a little banter about his being on Basie's band. When that ended a man approached him and his group and said, "Hi, my name is Bob Ross. You guys sounded pretty good. I own the Rex Hotel across the street. I'd like to buy you guys lunch and a couple of drinks there." Sam thanked him, and across the street they went.

Sam says, "We walk in and I see that the place is dilapidated; there were derelicts sucking up beer. We sat, and Bob Ross sat with us, and we ordered food. It was sandwiches, burgers, and beer. Bob Ross said, 'What would it take to get you guys to play here?' I said, 'Here? I don't think there'd be too many jazz fans here.' Bob Ross said, 'No, I'd expect you, your group, to bring them in, that's why I wanted to talk to you.' I told him that we had played for a couple of hours and gotten a hundred bucks apiece. Bob Ross said, 'Okay, done, you can start next Friday night.' "

Later on, the group had an evening gig, and another the next day. Sam crashed at Kirk McDonald's house, who at the time lived in Toronto. Sam didn't want to drive back and forth. The following week he drove up for the Rex Hotel gig. Sam says, "Evidently Bob Ross put something in the paper because a few people were there, and more were coming in. The derelicts were still there, but on the outer tables. Thirty or so people sat at tables in front, ready to listen to the music. We played, and our drinks were free."

Bob Ross paid them and asked about next Friday and Saturday. Sam said, "Why not?" The next Friday more people were there. Sam told me, "I mention this gig because now the Rex Hotel is the jazz place in Toronto and my group put it on the map, and Bob knows it. Anytime I wanted work there, all he needed was a few weeks' notice because he's booked solid. Someone books music all the time, day and night. The place is a phenomenon, a gold mine! Someone offered him a couple of million for the spot, an offer he refused. It became a pretty hip place, and they started hiring Pat LaBarbara and other good local players, and they're still doing it."

"Toronto was great to me," says Sam. "I was there thirteen years and never had to work a day job. I made a living playing the trumpet. But then, around 1988, when I'm fifty-eight years old, synthesizers, electronic things are everywhere. Work was becoming sparse. Sparse? It dried up."

For Sam, jazz gigs were few, and other gigs were just a necessity, but he was now getting pension money. He was losing interest in many things. He'd drive to Buffalo to see guys he knew. "My daughter lives there, as does my son, Chris. Andrew lives in Toronto. My first son, Michael, who stayed in Vegas, now lives in Seattle, Washington. Everyone is spread out."

In Buffalo, Sam called Dennis Tribuzzi, a fine lead trumpet player. They started rehearsing a trumpet section thing, and then Sam called others. Joe Baudo came in on piano, Soon, it was becoming a big band. Because of Baudo's orchestrations and big band arrangements, he evolved into the leader. They rehearsed regularly at the Colored Musician's Club on Broadway, but suddenly the Club wanted to charge Joe for the space.

In the past, Sam had gigged with tenor man Sam Falzone at The Sportsmen's on Amherst Street in Black Rock. Sam says, "I knew Dwane Hall, the owner. I asked him if a big band could come in at noon every Tuesday to rehearse for a few hours. He said, 'Sure, Sam, okay.' " Word spread, and people started attending the rehearsals. Before long a Black Rock musical monster was created, and musicians were playing a gig for free drinks, but Baudo and Sam were the only ones drinking. Joe did that 50-50 drawing to get the band a few bucks. Sam had dental problems and left the band. Playing was painful.

A couple of years ago Steve McDade, a great trumpet player in Toronto, called Sam. He said, "Sam, we want to celebrate your life in Toronto at the Rex Jazz and Blues Bar. I spoke with the owner and he's all for it, so when can you do it?" Sam says, "I was taken aback by this. We set up a date. At the time I was still rehearsing at The Sportsmen's. On a break I mentioned it to the guys, and someone said, 'We should all go up there.' So, a bunch of Buffalo guys, my good friends, Louie Marinaccio, Al Wallach,

Joe Parisi, Jim Bohm, Ray Chamberlain, Louie Marino, Richie Merlo, Don Angelo, Joe Baudo, and Phil Nyhuis, chartered a bus and picked me up at my home in Fort Erie. I can't remember all the names. I hope I don't offend anybody by that. We had a great time on the bus with lots of beer. I told a few stories and we had many laughs. We arrived in Toronto, and in front of the Rex Hotel I saw a big sign that said, 'Celebrating Sam Noto.' We entered, and I couldn't believe my eyes. The club was mobbed! It was great. Ten trumpet players started playing my charts. It was fantastic. Great night. After it ended, McDade handed me a big bunch of money. They had charged admission. I tried paying some of the musicians, but nobody would take any money. That was a great honor for me."

In a city that wasn't his hometown, Torontonians treated Sam admirably. From them he felt much respect. Every Canadian trumpet man there that day, all good players, told him how much he inspired them. Sam was astounded by it all. He wondered about that veneration, that sincere treatment for months. In retrospect, Sam Noto gave much to Buffalo, his city of birth, a place where he created two jazz clubs; Renaissance I, where he led a great local jazz band, and Renaissance II, where he brought in nationally known jazz attractions. Unfortunately, in Buffalo Sam Noto's efforts to advance an American art form went ignored.

The old truism "Prophets have honor all over the Earth, except in the village where they were born." For this writer who has known Sam since 1949 or 50, that axiom comes to mind after meeting, prodding, interviewing, hearing audiotapes, and listening to Sam Noto. He is a jazz prophet whose best music was played in Buffalo, and for the most part it went unnoticed, or, as he says, "fluffed off."

Years ago, on Pearl Street at Renaissance I, the late Louie Marinaccio tape recorded Sam with the late guitarist Ray Chamberlain, drummer Al Checchi, and with Tom and Joe Azarello on piano and bass. The music from one of those nights became a CD entitled Sam Noto Renaissance. Sam isn't a braggart and doesn't come off as one, but I've listened to the 1965 CD repeatedly and I love it. Through the years I've been fortunate to dialogue with some who were present in those Renaissance I nights and whose applause was often recorded. They agree; Sam played his heart out. He was a jazz detective, finding clues in an intricate maze of musical keys, many in high speed, high powered but non-felonious elegant chord progressions. Upon finishing his solo, no one applauded. Niente! I've known Ray Chamberlain for decades, having played with him in abundant venues. When Ray soloed— and finished—and I'm not taking anything from Ray, he played beautifully, he was applauded.

In Buffalo, for many years Sam Noto was taken for granted. I sensed he too sensed that, and I avoided asking him. Finally, it's as if he knows he can't perform here anymore and doesn't think he should.

In Toronto, Sam starred with Boss Brass, played jazz gigs, and, as we know, was later celebrated there. Sam says, "Buffalo see me, stares and says, Sam Noto? What the fuck? You're still here? Believe me, it's offensive." It's true. The place you leave is not the place to which you return. It's also true you can't go home again. Once you do, and if what you put out isn't accepted, what else can you do? When Sam lived in a different, bigger, better city with a progressive population—in a different country—a melting pot where jazz didn't originate, the people think he epitomizes jazz. Sam says, "You're back home, a place where you tried keeping jazz alive, and it's 'Not you again.' That's when you know you've failed, and it's beyond depressing. Through the years you realize who your real friends are.

"When I was in LA with Boss Brass I was a bad boy. Don and Rose Menza took me in and cared for me, big time. They were a Godsend. I could have died if not for them. On the other hand, when I was in Vegas, other people, friends, a family on their way to Los Angeles came to my home and stayed with us for several days. I fed them, drove them around the city, the whole thing. When they visit Buffalo, they don't call me! That offended me. More so, after learning on Facebook that my so-called friend was in town, no phone call. Nothing! It's like I'm not here, but I know he was. I know some people are not as passionate or caring as others. I agree with that. But sometimes you scratch your head and say, 'What's going on?' "

Late in 1989, Don Menza called Sam from LA. "Sam, come to New Orleans. I'm doing a professional video of my stuff. It will be you, me, Cedar Walton on piano, a drummer, and a bass player."

Menza sent Sam the plane ticket. Sam flew to New Orleans and checked into a little, old, and quaint hotel on Bourbon Street. They had that night off and were to rehearse the next afternoon. Needless to say, they were like two drunken sailors walking up and down Bourbon Street hitting every bar, drinking tequilas, beer, and eating oysters and finger food that made New Orleans famous. When they returned to the hotel they were stuffed. Sam said, "That first day was a gas. I slept, got up the next afternoon, and went to the rehearsal at Lulu's. We rehearsed, and cameramen were rehearsing the video they would shoot. Then we had a few hours off. We ate at a fine restaurant. When we returned, Lulu's was mobbed with musicians and jazz fans. A scholastic jazz competition was going on, and people we knew from all over the country were there as adjudicators; Bobby Shew, Don Rader, who I replaced in Basie's band, even Jeff Jarvis from Buffalo was there. We played the gig, and it went off well and was well received. Menza did some interviews, and they had the band playing. It was a professional video. It was Menza's thing. You can see much of that video, Don Menza in New Orleans, on my website and on YouTube. Menza gave me a thousand dollars and a ticket to get back home.

"One day I'm in Fort Erie commuting on occasion to Toronto when I get a call from Chuck Mangione who had a tour coming up and was using all upstate groups, like James Moody's band and the Nat Adderly Group. Chuck says his piano playing brother, Gap, is going to lead a sextet with stops up and down the New York State Thruway; Buffalo, Rochester, Syracuse, Watertown, Rome. I don't know if it went to Albany, but musicians would spend several days in each spot playing jazz. The tour was to be for three weeks, and Gap would lead the group I was in along with Joe Romano and Larry Covelli. He asked if I was interested. Of course I was, especially with Joe Romano involved. We were pretty tight, musically and otherwise. Chuck Mangione said, 'The gig pays $1,800 a week and the motels are taken care of.' I said, 'Okay, beautiful.' A few days later Chuck calls again. 'Sam, I've got good news and bad news. My brother will not be on the band you're in. I want you as a leader and I'll get another piano player. The good news is that you'll get double pay. You'll be making $3,600 a week.' Me! I'd never made that kind of money in my life. We start the tour and we're playing the towns. We played Buffalo. We played Rochester for a few days, then Syracuse and Rome where we had a good time, and many came to hear us. The club owner had us for dinner the nights we were there. In other cities, most of the time, not many people showed up. Chuck wasn't bugged when we talked about it on the phone. I'd say, 'Nobody's showing up for these gigs. Will you be able to pay?' He'd say, 'Don't worry Sam, just play, have fun, you'll get the bread.' That's how the whole tour went. It ended three weeks later at Shea's Buffalo Theater with all the musicians involved as a last concert. Chuck Mangione's big band with strings, French horns, and percussion playing the music that made him famous. I think that was '89 or '90."

DAMN YANKEES, DAMN STATE TAX

"In Buffalo it was odds and ends again with a gig here and there, and occasionally one in Toronto, but I sensed things were really slowing down. Lon Gormley was booking Broadway road shows at Shea's Buffalo. She called me for Damn Yankees with Jerry Lewis. Ang Callea was on the gig. We went into the pit and played a week. It was the usual two shows on Wednesday and on Saturday, but a whole week. We had a nice pit band. Come payday, everybody gets paid but me. I told Lon. We went to the paymaster who wants to know my name. I told him, and he said, 'New York State Tax people have confiscated your paycheck. They said you owe them $7,400.' I said, 'What? What are you talking about? I don't owe them any money.' He said it was about some tour and you made $3,600 a week. The State thinks I'm making that kind of money all year! They billed me, but I live in Canada, and I never got the mail. I was livid! I called Joe Carlisi who said he'd look into it. I can't owe that much for taxes. Luckily, Joe had it knocked down to $4,100. It's a good thing I banked that money because now I'm giving it to the State. So, there I was, no income, and odds and ends again. That was a drag. Funny I remembered that because I blocked it out of my mind, I was so bugged about it."

FREDDIE HUBBARD AND WOODY SHAW

In late 1991 or early '92, Menza called. "Sam, we're doing a one-week gig with Louie Bellson at the Blue Note in New York City. It pays a thousand bucks, but you must get there on your own, fend for yourself—find a place to stay and pay for your own food." Sam says, "I took the train, the Empire Express that stopped four times but was inexpensive. John Hasselback had a friend, Wally Fogg, who lived in New York. John communicated with Wally and arranged for me to stay at his pad. Menza stayed with Joe Rocasanno, a friend who lived at the Manhattan Plaza on 48th Street in midtown with a beautiful view of the city. To live there you had to be in the Arts. Menza cooked dinner a few times, and each time I was invited. Wally's pad was in Hell's Kitchen, around 54th and Eighth Avenue, where it's really, really weird. After the gig I'd take a cab there. The building didn't have an elevator, so I walked up five flights of stairs. Wally's pad didn't have furniture, only a mattress on the kitchen floor, and that's where I slept. Well, beggars can't be choosers, right? I appreciated John Hasselback's help in getting Wally to take me in. But I did tell Menza that Wally's pad was the worst. In contrast, the Blue Note gig was great. There were two bands, Louie's Quintet and alto man Phil Woods' band with a great trombone player. We played two forty-five minute shows a night. We'd break, and Phil's group would come out. A lot of people came to hear us. Freddie Hubbard, Ira Gittler, the writer, and lots of musicians. I never played under those circumstances. I played with big bands in New York, but never in a small jazz setting. So that was quite exciting for me. Freddie Hubbard invited me to his table. He said, 'You sound great, man.' Then he said, 'Sam, do you remember that time in Chicago when we had that trumpet battle?' I said, 'That was Rochester, Freddie, that wasn't Chicago. After that we were even friendlier.' "

Seeing Freddie Hubbard in the audience and his recalling the Rochester incident brought another story to Sam's mind. "It was probably 1984, a Wednesday night, when I was still in Toronto. While having my before-dinner drink and watching TV, I get a phone call from Kate Roach, a Toronto booking agent. Kate went with a tenor player I knew. She asked, 'What are you doing tonight, and don't think I'm trying to make out with you. I'm calling because I booked Woody Shaw and Joe Henderson for a two-trumpet thing at a club with Jerry Fuller on drums, Gary Williamson, piano, and Neil Swainson on bass, but Henderson can't be there. I thought you'd like to play with Woody who I talked to, and who said it was cool. The gig pays two hundred a night for two nights.' I said, 'If it's okay with Woody, I'll do it.' I went there and Kate introduced me to Woody whose reputation I knew, but I didn't know him personally except that he was one of the best jazz trumpet players around. I heard that he cleaned up his act and was off drugs and was sounding good, and he was almost blind, legally blind. Before we played, Woody introduced me to his girl, and she said, 'Sam Noto, eh? Sicilian?' I said, 'Yeah.' She said, 'So am I.' She opened her purse and pulled out a mickey of booze. 'Here, take a swig of this and get prepared for what's going to happen.' So, I took a swig. I'm in the wings and while over the mike someone is announcing that Woody and I are about to play, Woody slips a pill into my hand. I asked what it was, and he said, 'Ginseng, man. Health food.' I swallowed it. We went out and we played standards. I didn't know his charts and he didn't have them on paper, so we played tunes we both knew and were enjoying it. The last tune of the set was 'All the Things You Are.' Woody played it beautifully. He was a sensational player. Then I played. I happened to hit a pretty good solo, after which we got applause. People loved the two-trumpet thing. So, Woody said, 'We're taking a short break.' We walk off the stand and he said, 'Sam, walk me off, man.' So, I had him by the arm and as we're walking into the wings he said, 'By the way, no more ginseng for you. Man, after your solo on 'All the Things You Are' I'm not giving you no more ginseng.' Those two nights with Woody, we hit it off. When the gig ended I'm home, and I get a call to go to a downtown piano bar; Woody's there and wants to talk to me. I arrive, and Woody says, 'How would you like to go to Europe with me to do the two-trumpet thing?' I said, 'Fantastic.' He asked me if I had a passport. I asked him when the gig was. He said it was in three or four weeks. Knowing how long you wait for a passport, I went to the Canadian Consulate. I told them what an opportunity Woody Shaw has given me. I received a passport in a few weeks. That was unheard of. While I'm waiting for Woody to call, I learned he was back in New York, back on drugs, and missed the whole tour. It would have been a great thing for me to play with him. He was such a fantastic player. I would have learned so much.

"Around that time, I get a call for a gig from the great Canadian pianist, Norm Amadio. His group had a female singer they were playing for in Grenada. I took an Airport limo to Toronto, met the guys, and flew to Grenada. It was January. Grenada is pretty close to the Equator, so it was like a vacation. We had about four, five days there. We only did one concert and backed up the Grenadian singer. They put us up in a hotel, fed us, and treated us like kings. Grenada is a beautiful island.

"About the same time, Menza calls from California; Louis Bellson wants to put a quintet together to play in Fano, Italy, for their first jazz festival ever, and on the Adriatic Sea. We met in New York, flew to Rome, got on a chartered bus, and drove to Fano, about ninety minutes from Rome across the boot. We played two gigs; one at night and one the next day on the beach at two in the afternoon. Many people were on that show; trumpeter Roy Hargrove, and the old clarinet player, Tony Scott. We walked two blocks from our hotel to a restaurant where the festival promoter, an Italian guy, paid for anything we ordered. Louie, Don, me, and the piano man, Mike Abene, were having dinner, and in came Roy Hargrove, and his group. They sat at a nearby table. Roy sat with his feet up on a chair like a schmuck. A guy in his group noticed Louis Bellson and said to Roy, 'Louis Bellson is at the next table. You should go over and pay your respects.' Hargrove said, 'I don't know him. What the hell's he gonna to do for me?' To tell you the truth, I felt like getting up and punching him in the mouth. What an attitude. Some people think they're way better than what they are. There were many highlights on that festival, but Hargrove's arrogance was the lowlight. It was so infuriating. Returning to the States I boarded an Air Italia plane in Rome. I was in the last seat in the last row in the tail end, and I felt lots of turbulence. It was hot, crowded, horrible, and I'm waiting forever for the drink cart. When we landed, the pilot hit the ground so hard the overhead bins burst open; men women and children were screaming. It was crazy, scary, like a bad movie; horrible. The food? It was the absolute worst. Air Italia? Who'd believe it? But in spite of that nonsense, all I thought about in the air was the Fano concert, and what we played from Side Track. The audience went wild, they loved it."

For the record, I've listened and listened to Side Track, the aforementioned Louie Bellson CD. To my ears that CD, album, record, call it what you will, contains some of the best jazz ever recorded. As a musician who has played jazz and listened to it for seventy plus years, Side Track ranks with the best, whoever the best are, or may be. I've always maintained once we discover who "they" are, our lives continue uninterrupted. Leonard Feather was correct in his appraisal of Sam Noto's ability, and his alluding to the fact that not many have heard Sam Noto. Those that haven't, must listen long and hard to Side Track, a CD that should be required listening in any venue of higher education that offers jazz studies. Not to diminish Menza who is superb on Side Track, but I as a trumpet player listening to Noto's work was more than astonished. He is remarkably superb. To say otherwise would be a huge understatement. Noto's articulation, his musical inner self personifies the essence of jazz, its purity, integrity, and metaphorical intelligence, which in and of itself is a personal attitude. The life he led, and still lives, is that of a totally dedicated musician whose inventive heart, a genius (a word I choose carefully) filled with a desire without exception to play the music he loves, a music many don't understand. One must remember, Sam Noto's jazz trumpet virtuosity, his incredible sound was obscured by many challenges and absurdities; driving dump trucks, making batteries, and the ignorance of strippers. That aside, in any venue, Royal Albert Hall, the Blue Note, or the Palace Burlesk, his musicality, always of the highest caliber, brought him jazz cult status. The noted jazz journalist Steve Cerra, in writing about Stan Kenton's recording of Back to Balboa said, "It was that album that introduced me to Sam Noto's beautiful sound in the jazz trumpet chair."

EPILOGUE: THE AUTHOR, AND THE PASSION OF SAM NOTO

"Love is a destructive vapor arising from an educated and discerning conception of adolescent passion and animal affection." That inscription came to me via my dear, late, and lifelong friend Angelo Tona, a retired New York City judge who found it sixty-five years ago in a Reader's Digest magazine. I've not forgotten those words. What Sam Noto has done with his life, and the love he had for what he did, defies description. This was, and still is, a musically philosophical and contemplative artist of the highest order who since his early youth has nourished his soul with his music, and to this day, continues to do so.

As we now know, Sam's world entailed viable things filled with desire. In that domain he is enthusiastically allied with past late-greats; Charlie Parker, and trumpeters Dizzy Gillespie and Fats Navarro. He is immersed in his art and lived his own Shangri-La, an earthly utopian paradise isolated from intrusion.

The passionate get excited. They can be sullen as well, and through passion they have a clear meaning of their life purpose. For various motives, they give less importance to what others do, and risk more for the goal they deem to be highest. They abhor what is not in their sphere, what isn't sensible; all else vanishes from their lives. Sam Noto was his own passion. He never saw it as separate from his own persona. He couldn't equalize chaos and tranquility. As was the case with the brilliance of the late Miles Davis, another of Sam's storied counterparts.

In the mid '80s, Sam, after a gig in Ottawa, Ontario, stayed at tenor man Kirk McDonald's house. By then, Kirk was a Royal Canadian Mounted Police Officer and lived there. It was five in the morning and the phone rang. Kirk woke up, picked up the phone, and said, "Hello." He listened, gave the phone to Sam, and said, "It's your wife." Sam, into the phone, said, "Arleen, what is it? Did something happen?" She said, "Sam, did Miles Davis get in touch with you?" Sam said, "Miles Davis? What are you talking about?" She said, "Arnie Chycoski called and said Miles Davis was calling people all over Toronto trying to get in touch with you. He left a NYC number for you to call." Arleen gave Sam the number, and he wrote it on a piece of paper. Kirk asked, "Is everything okay?" Sam said, "Yes" and told him about Arnie's phone call. Kirk said, "Call the number." Sam said, "No, it must be a prank. It's gotta be. I'm not doing that." Kirk said, "Sam, Arnie's a dear friend of yours, your mate in The Boss Brass, you and he are two of the best trumpet players in the country; he wouldn't do that to you, you know that. Give me the number, I'll call."

The phone number was that of the New York City hotel where Miles Davis did in fact reside. Kirk dialed the number and the phone rang. A woman who answered said, "Who's calling?" Kirk said, "Sam Noto for Miles Davis." The woman said, "Just a minute." She returned and said, "Miles isn't taking any calls." Sam said, "By then it was six in the morning. Kirk calls the number again, but now he tells the woman who answers that he's Tony Williams, Miles' drummer. Again, the woman said, 'Miles isn't taking any calls.' Sam says, "I never learned what that was about. I don't know if it was Miles or someone playing a bad joke."

Sam Noto knew Miles Davis. They were friends. In 1965, in Buffalo, for one week during the last days of the Towne Casino, Sam, in Don Menza's band, played opposite Miles Davis's group that included Herbie Hancock, George Coleman, and Tony Williams. Sam says, "Early in the week Miles is playing, and I'm off to the side digging him. Miles leaves the stand, comes over to me and asks, 'Do you like the way Tony Williams plays?' I said, 'Yeah, man, he can play!' Miles looks at me and says, 'Do you like the way George Coleman plays?' And I say, 'Oh yeah, George Coleman is great. I dig him.' When I said that, Miles looked me straight in the eye, and said, 'Tony Williams doesn't like the way George plays.' With that he went back to the bandstand.

"Miles's last night was on a Saturday. His Harmon mute was defective, and he asked if he could use mine. I said he could. Our group worked Monday to Saturday and we were off Sunday. Miles's group played Tuesday to Sunday and would leave town the next day, Monday. As Sunday night ended, Miles watched as I put the mute away. He said, 'Where are you going with the mute? I'm not going to steal your mute man.' I left it with him. I had to be back Monday night, so if he absconded with it I can always say, 'Miles Davis stole my mute,' if not, no harm done. When I returned it was there."

In closing these pages Sam Noto says, "Early in this work I spoke respectfully of Mr. Norman Weis, my high school music teacher. In school, when I played I puffed my cheeks. That upset Mr. Weis who wanted me to stop. He'd say, 'Sam, don't puff, that isn't the way to play, that's not prim and proper.' In retrospect, I only took a few private lessons, and could be described as self-taught. I didn't know, or want to know, about prim and proper. When I started playing, and was soon exposed to Bird and Dizzy, I quickly learned they weren't prim and proper but were great players who took chances and put pure and honest passion into their music. As far as I'm concerned, passion is what you need, never mind not puffing! I said to myself, 'This is the way I want to play, like Bird and Dizzy.' I didn't care much about discipline. That's the thing. Otherwise, it's sterile. Ever since that day many years ago in Whiteman's Song Shop, I knew Bird and Dizzy were where it was at, and that is how I wanted to play. I disregarded some of the rules Mr. Weis laid down. I may have been a misfit, but through the years, so were the jazz artists who inspired me and who created an internal musical rage I embraced with my heart, and with all of my love. I know I did it the way they did.

"For possessing that similar passion, many great jazz players destroyed their lives, as did Charlie Parker, my greatest inspiration. I never heard anybody play like that in my entire life, and I heard many great players. He did what he had to do and thought he had to get his thing across using heroin, a totally destructive drug that killed him at age thirty-five. Is that the way it was supposed to be? I don't know, and I don't have an answer. To get the passion sometimes, I had to maybe have a couple of drinks, relax, and get all the cobwebs out of my head, and bring the passion back. Sometimes you go overboard, and you have too many 'couple of drinks,' and then you sound rotten, and you get messy with yourself. I've seen a lot of guys do heavy things and destroy themselves. Freddie Hubbard was a great player, but he got so wound up with coke. I went to hear him in Toronto, and he couldn't play the melody to 'Funny Valentine' until his guy showed up, and he went into the john and did his thing, he came out, and sounded great. I'm not condoning or putting anything up or down, I'm saying that the people who did the great things that inspired me musically did it their way. I had no control over what they used to arrive there. I love jazz, and everything about it, still do. If you talk to anyone who's really serious about this kind of music, they'll tell you, you have to do whatever it takes to get your thing out.

"In the early '90s when we left Toronto, life there was not only expensive but also uneventful. I was older and in a metropolis where the regime has changed and younger musicians are the ones hired. That's usual, it's par for the course. That's what happens when you're a freelance musician; a sideman. You become old hat, no matter how good or bad you're playing. People change. The older ones don't come out, and the young ones don't know or care to know who you are; they're into a different kind of what they call music. It gets uneventful, and you think of visiting the Tomb of the Unknown Jazz Musician. All kind of memories go through your mind. That's when you begin to wonder. I'm at an age now where how long can you go? We all know that. But certain things stay with you and stick in your craw. The song Mr. Sinatra sang, yeah, you did it your way, but regrets I have a few. I have more than a few. I made some bad decisions. I paid dues for that through my wife, and people dear to me. I moved around so much. But my kids are cool. Jennifer, as stated earlier, is here. Michael lives in Seattle, Chris in Toronto, and Andrew lives in Buffalo. You question and wonder about your decisions, your priorities, and those you may have hurt. So, aging you get nostalgic, screwed up, and this stuff fills your head. It's maybe an occupational hazard? Do I know? No, I don't know! How could I? I'm only a sideman."

Poet Philip Larkin writing on jazz musicians of the early 1940s:

"Men whose first coronary is coming like Christmas; who drift, loaded helplessly with commitments, and obligations, and necessary observances, into the darkening avenues of age, and incapacity, deserted by everything that once made life sweet."

ANOTHER NOTE

I asked Don Angelo, a friend of many years, who is a long-time radio industry person and member of the Buffalo Hall of Fame Broadcasters to write "My Trumpet Teacher' about his personal Noto experience. Don agreed and also listed, to his expert knowledge, all of Sam Noto's known recorded solo work.

My Trumpet Teacher

In the mid-1950s I was a sixteen-year-old trumpet player when I discovered Sam Noto, who at the time was my West Side neighbor and my soon-to-be idol. I was in Grover Cleveland High School's all-star dance band, and at the time we were preparing for the New York State High School Band Competition. Our teacher, Norman Weis (who taught Sam Noto at a different high school) loaded us onto a bus to Bath, New York, where high school dance bands statewide, including New York City, would compete for best band, and we were voted best. All fourteen of us influenced by the West Side musical culture thought we were ready to join the Stan Kenton Orchestra.

It was then that we discovered a local daily radio show on WHLD from three to six in the afternoon. After school, my good pal, tenor sax man Phil DiRe, and I would meet our buddy Frank Merlino, a recent recipient of a NYS driver's license. We drove around listening to this newly discovered music introduced by Joe

Rico, a DJ and really cool cat who played Stan Kenton records that featured Sam Noto. Rico became one of America's top jazz DJs. His popularity was so strong Stan Kenton commissioned composer Gene Rowland to write a theme for Rico and called it "Jump for Joe." It became Joe Rico's life-long theme.

While Rico was being lionized by Kenton, I lionized Sam Noto. I'm happy to say I was one of his trumpet students when he was home between Kenton tours, and we became fast friends.

Many decades later that friendship still exists. Today, Sam Noto, my childhood idol, teacher, and friend and I are on a fascinating quest exploring the trumpets of the world, and the holy grail of horns. We've tested and modified trumpet mouthpieces. We've experimented with different rims, bowls, back-bores, bells and bell flare sizes, lead-pipes, and finishes. In working with brass, copper, gold plate, silver, and lacquer, we seek to find the ideal balance suitable for older trumpet and brass players, more prone than other musicians in terms of aging. So, who best to conduct this mundane study, as well as searching for the magic grail that older retired players with knowledge, experience, and time? Us! That's what we do. It may sound crazy, but it's fun, it keeps us young and out of trouble. I love hanging out with Sam Noto, my long-ago trumpet teacher and jazz legend.

SAM NOTO DISCOGRAPHY

Stan Kenton: Showcase (Capitol 1954)
Capitol Classics Volume 2 (Capitol 1954)
Contemporary Concepts (Capitol 1955)
Kenton in Hi-Fi (Capitol 1956)
Cuban Fire (Capitol 1956)
Rendezvous with Kenton (Capitol 1957)
Back to Balboa (Capitol 1958)
Frank Rosolino: Kenton Presents Jazz (Capitol 1954, 1956)
Count Basie: Pop Goes the Basie (Reprise 1965)
The Happiest Millionaire (Coliseum 1967)
Half a Sixpence (Dot 1967)
Sam Noto: Sam Noto Live at the Renaissance (SLR 1966)
Red Rodney: Superbop (Muse 1974)
Entrance! (Xanadu 1975)
Act One (Xanadu 1975)
Rob McConnell: The Jazz Album (Seabreese 1976)
Dexter Gordon: Silver Blue (Xanadu 1976)
True Blue (Xanadu 1976)
Notes to You (Xanadu 1977)
Noto-Riety (Xanadu 1978)
Kenny Drew: For Sure (Xanadu 1978)
Live in Digital (Sea Breese 1980)
Hip Pocket (Fresh Sound 1981)
Side Track (Louie Bellson 1980)
Don Menza: Live at Carmelo's (Fresh Sound 1981)
2-4-5 (Unisso 1987)
Night Flight (Sea Breese 1993)
Now Here This (Supermono 1999)

ABOUT THE AUTHOR

Joey Giambra was born in the lower West Side of Buffalo, New York, in 1933 of Sicilian immigrant parents. Rising from the poverty of the day, he is a Jazz trumpeter, singer, lyricist, poet, band leader, gourmet chef, author, playwright, and a twenty-year veteran of the Buffalo Police Force. When not writing, he continues to perform in theatres and clubs.

Made in the USA
Columbia, SC
23 September 2018